A Potter's Guide to Raw Glazing and Oil Firing

OTHER PUBLICATIONS BY DENNIS PARKS:

CRAFT REVIEW
"Chicago Area," in *Craft Horizons*

CRAFT ARTICLES
"Paul Soldner," in *Craft Horizons*
"Single-Fire Glazing," in *Studio Potter*
"Fired Free," in *Studio Potter*
"Dust Glazing," in *Ceramics Monthly*
"Single-Fire Glazing," in *Ceramic Review* (London)
"Single-Fire Glazing," in *New Zealand Potter*
"Starting a Pottery School," in *Goodfellow Review of Crafts*

NONFICTION (General)
"Snake, The Lawyer," in *Cavalier*

POETRY
Poems in *Spectrum* and *Carolina Quarterly*

A Potter's Guide to Raw Glazing and Oil Firing

DENNIS PARKS

CHARLES SCRIBNER'S SONS / NEW YORK

Copyright © 1980 Dennis Parks

Library of Congress Cataloging in Publication Data
Parks, Dennis.
  A potter's guide to raw glazing and oil firing.
  1. Pottery craft. 2. Glazing (Ceramics).
I. Title.
TT920.P37   738.1'43   79-17357
ISBN 0-684-16392-6

This book published simultaneously in
the United States of America and Canada.

Copyright under the Berne Convention.

All rights reserved. No part of this book
may be reproduced in any form without
the permission of Charles Scribner's Sons.

Printed in the United States of America.

1 3 5 7 9 11 13 15 17 19 Q/C 20 18 16 14 12 10 8 6 4 2

All photographs in this book are, unless otherwise credited, by the author.

On the jacket: "Landscape Plate VII," by the author. Stoneware. 1974. Diameter 12 inches (30.5 cm.). White slip applied to leather-hard clay, oxides and glaze applied to dry clay; fired with drainoil. Collection of Dennis J. Roberts. (*Photograph by Valerie Parks*)

"WHY DON'T YOU LOVE ME" by Hank Williams. © Copyright 1950 by Fred Rose Music, Inc. Copyright Renewed 1977. Jointly controlled in the U.S.A. by Fred Rose Music, Inc. and Aberbach Enterprises, Ltd. (Unichappell Music, administrator) Controlled outside the U.S.A. by Fred Rose Music, Inc. International Copyright Secured, Made in U.S.A. All rights reserved.

Specified material from *The Horse's Mouth* by Joyce Cary. © 1944 by Joyce Cary. Reprinted by permission of Harper & Row, Publishers, Inc.

To J.P.

ACKNOWLEDGMENTS

Following is a list of the persons who shared with me in letters their knowledge, experiences, photographs, drawings, and glaze recipes:

William C. Alexander
Bozeman, Montana
Jim Allen
Houston, Texas
Bennett Bean
Blairstown, New Jersey
Frank Boyden
Otis, Oregon
Max Braverman
Hope, New Jersey
Rosemary Capes
Vera, Almeria, Spain
Burt Cohen
Nelson, British Columbia, Canada
David Cornell
Talent, Oregon
Bill Creitz
Manning, Oregon
Suzi Curtis
Coxwold, York, Great Britain
Carla Damler
La Jara, New Mexico
Peter Dick
Coxwold, York, Great Britain
Roland DiSanza
Ely, Nevada
Tony Evans
Plymouth, Devonshire, Great Britain
Ray Gardiner
Yoxford, Suffolk, Great Britain
John Green
Portland, Oregon
Ken Hendry
Fort Collins, Colorado
Steven Hill
Kansas City, Missouri
Andrew Holden
South Tawton, Devonshire, Great Britain
Phyllis Ihrman
Farmington Hills, Michigan
Sandra Johnstone
Los Altos, California
Jonathan Chiswell Jones
Hailsham, E. Sussex, Great Britain
Carl J. Judson, Jr.
Fort Collins, Colorado
James E. Kerns
Cedar Falls, Iowa
Steve and Ann Kilborn
Ranchos de Taos, New Mexico
Andrew Lord
Rotterdam, Netherlands
Jere Lykins
Rome, Georgia
Richard Mackey
Alturas, California
Lynn G. Maddox
Portola Valley, California
McKensie Musick
Portland, Oregon
Olin Russum
Monkton, Maryland
Don and Isao Sanami/Morrill
Nova Scotia, Canada
Larry Shep
Arroyo Grande, California
Don and Marcia Skolnick-Simonson
Germantown, Maryland
Peter Sohngen
Memphis, Tennessee
Paul Soldner
Aspen, Colorado
Andrée Valley
Ann Arbor, Michigan
Betty Woodman
Boulder, Colorado

My thanks to all of you, and to the editors of *Ceramic Review* (London), *Ceramics Monthly, Studio Potter,* and *New Zealand Potter* for their encouragement in this project. Those glaze recipes designated "Courtesy of *Ceramic Review*" are reprinted, by kind permission of *Ceramic Review*, from the *Ceramic Review Book of Glaze Recipes.*

I am indebted to the Nevada State Council on the Arts for a grant that allowed me to neglect making pottery while writing this book.

My appreciation goes to Ron Moroni and Valerie Parks for their photography, and to Katy Hertel, Margaret Norman, and Valerie for the drawings; to Lois Parks for typing and retyping; to Arnold Schraer for proofreading; and to Julie for advice and criticism.

Finally, an apology to my sons—Ben and Greg—for my writing on weekends when I should have been out fishing with them, as I had promised.

Dennis Parks
Tuscarora, Nevada
October 1979

CONTENTS

1. **Introduction: "What Makes You Treat Me Like a Piece of Clay?"** 3
   On Starting a Pottery School... in the Middle of Nowhere on Next to Nothing 3
   Technical Innovations? 6
   Stopping the Bisque 8

2. **Raw Glazing: Single-Firing, Once-Firing, Etc.** 10
   A Brief Look at the History of Glazing 10
   Why Glaze? 12
   What Is Glaze? 13
   Theories and Methods of Making Glaze 14
   Raw Glaze Versus Bisque Glaze 17
   The Relationship Between Clay and Raw Glaze 17

3. **The Application and the Fire** 19
   Applying Glaze to Bone-Dry Clay 19
   Applying Glaze to Wet and Leather-Hard Clay 32
   Firing Only Once 37
   Glaze List 38

4. **Other Approaches: Variations in Single-Firing** 47
   Salt Glaze 47
   Self-Glazing Clay 53
   Terra Sigillata 55
   Terra Nigra 56

5. **Burning Drainoil** 58
   Why Not Fire with Drainoil? 58
   The Nature of Oil 58
   Oil Burners 66
   Setting Up a System to Burn Drainoil 74
   The Value of Adding Water to Oil 76
   The Oil-Fired Kiln 77
   An Idealized Firing Schedule 79

6. **Conclusion: The Kiln... and the Countryside** 82
   How to Build a Dirt-Cheap Kiln 82
   Stalking Wild Materials 95
   Notes 105
   Bibliography 106
   Sources of Hard-to-Find Equipment 108
   Index 109

'B-but, Mr Jimson, I w-want to be an artist.'

'Of course you do,' I said, 'everybody does once. But they get over it, thank God, like the measles and the chicken-pox. Go home and go to bed and take some hot lemonade and put on three blankets and sweat it out.'

'But Mr J-Jimson, there must be artists.'

'Yes, and lunatics and lepers, but why go and live in an asylum before you're sent for? If you find life a bit dull at home,' I said, 'and want to amuse yourself, put a stick of dynamite in the kitchen fire, or shoot a policeman. Volunteer for a test pilot, or dive off Tower Bridge with five bobs' worth of roman candles in each pocket. You'd get twice the fun at about one-tenth of the risk.'

—Joyce Cary, *The Horse's Mouth*

A Potter's Guide to Raw Glazing and Oil Firing

1. View from Tuscarora looking east toward the Independence Mountains. (*Valerie Parks*)

CHAPTER 1

Introduction: "What Makes You Treat Me Like a Piece of Clay?" —HANK WILLIAMS

**ON STARTING A POTTERY SCHOOL...
IN THE MIDDLE OF NOWHERE
ON NEXT TO NOTHING**

Even total strangers visiting my studio finally get around to the question, "How did you discover Tuscarora?" I always try to change the subject since the answer is rambling and a little embarrassing. (Columbus must have felt similarly when asked about how he stumbled onto America.)

I got lost. I resorted to what Europeans and Americans have traditionally done in confusion—move west. When that does not help, you just keep moving.

Tuscarora, Nevada, where I finally settled, has a population of sixteen. From the valley the town looks like a handful of dice rolled up on the side of a mountain, stuck there on some sagebrush. At the turn of the century there were still gold and silver here. Elevation: 6,400 feet. Distances: San Francisco—600 miles; Los Angeles—700 miles. The closest grocery store is in Elko, 52 miles south.

This is beautiful country, unless you have an obsession with trees. There are a few in the canyons: willows, aspens, and cottonwoods. You notice them only in the fall when the leaves begin to die, turning yellow, orange, and red—from a distance like bright balls on the gray-green felt of sagebrush. The mountains loom behind. Rocks pushed to the surface at the peaks. Most of the year these are sculptors' mountains and painters' skies.

Before I settled here I had lived half my life in the suburbs of Washington, D.C.; gone to colleges in New Jersey, Switzerland, North Carolina, Iowa, and California. I spent two years teaching college in Illinois, then another four doing the same in the Los Angeles Basin, and lived a few other places for reasons I have forgotten.

Tuscarora tickled that fantasy of living the pastoral life where one is spontaneously stimulated and inspired—by sunrises, digging in the garden, slopping the pigs, seeing your wife milking the goats, watching your sons grow so rapidly that you are puzzled why you are not aging proportionately.

My good urban friends had many times tried to humor me through what they thought was an attack or an overdose of rural. But it was no use. With me a placebo works as well, maybe better, than the real medicine. I believed in Tuscarora before I drove up the road.

In our culture it is simple to understand someone in search of a better life giving up smoking, taking up jogging, and enrolling in Yoga. But a person who refuses tenure, quits a soft teaching job, and moves his family to an abandoned mining camp is rightfully suspect. The few who question me sympathetically, sometimes with a twitch of envy, are usually saying "Family money" under their breath.

That is a persistent, pernicious myth which we all live with, "If I only had his money, I'd do what I want." The opposite is more consistent: persons with money do not know what they want to do with it.

I am independently poor. The second son born to a civil servant and an elementary school teacher. I enjoyed what by global standards would be considered a soft and indulgent childhood. By mid-century American values, I grew up epicenter middle class. The cultural message was clear: grow up, get educated, and find a good job. My reaction to this environment was to develop an abnormal, obsessive fear of security, of being comfortable, serene, and bored: of being grown-up, static, stable, consistent, and dependable. It was fright, not money nor courage pushed me up the mountain. Of course, now that I am here I can generate many more palpable reasons for staying.

To supplement my income as a potter, my wife, Julie, and I purchased the only hotel in Tuscarora. It cost the equivalent of what my withholding taxes had been the year before. I started taking in students. At first it was just two or three referred by their teachers who were sympathetic to what I was trying. For the last couple of years students have been coming from all over the United States. The minimum stay is one month, but most stay for a full semester. Only eight are accepted. Now and then there is a waiting list.

Of course making it work was not that simple. During the six years while I was an assistant professor of art here and there, I had no summer vacations. I advertised and then taught summer workshops in Tuscarora. My special thanks go to the early students who came so far, not exactly certain what benefit they were going to get from the experience. We prospected for native materials, dug and processed our clay, constructed kick wheels, and built kilns. When it looked as if existing structures were too small, these students helped erect new studios.

In the spring of 1974, after I had spent my sabbatical and a leave of absence in Tuscarora, I mailed a letter to California resigning my college position. This was twelve years after Julie and I first saw the town. We had stood, each holding a kid in diapers, and agreed Tuscarora would be a good place to set them down. I was not impulsive, though many times daydreaming through faculty meetings, I wished I had the abandon to be. By the time I decided, "If we don't go now we'll never make the break," our boys were teenagers.

The original Tuscarora Pottery School studio was a mid-nineteenth-century carriage shop with a worrisome lean to the southeast. We worked there for four summers until 1970 when the owner reclaimed it for his own use. The next three years we were set up in and around my refurbished chicken house. It was during the last summer there that we built a geodesic dome, 28 feet in diameter, which has since been the students' studio.

Our glaze room was an eight-by-sixteen-foot woodshed, inadequate in size and lighting. So as soon as the dome was finished and paid for, I started drawing up ideas for another structure. In the summer of 1975 we dug foundation holes and started construction on what will someday be a two-storey studio, eighteen by forty-four, with a glaze room, two studios, and a storage area.

Our construction schedule moves at a speed dependent on the financial health of the school. Though we have our nonprofit status with the I.R.S. (I am a poor fund raiser), our capital expenses' budget comes out of the students' fees. With enrollment of only eight, there is not much left after buying food, clay, chemicals, and firebricks.

Economy is one of the subjects my students learn. To circumvent salaries for a cook and janitor, we have a two-day rotating chore list. All of us take turns cooking meals, washing dishes, sweeping, and mopping. During the summers we raise vegetables organically, with a boost from the free manure off the neighboring ranches. Our milk is from three Nubian goats, eggs from our Rhode Island Reds, and fresh meat from New Zealand White rabbits, Peking ducks, and a garbage-fed pig. My sons

2. The "Hotel." (*Ron Moroni*)

3. Tuscarora Pottery School studios. (*Ron Moroni*)

and I hunt mule deer in the fall, and almost everyone gets into fishing—in the streams or through the ice.

This saving-and-sharing attitude steps up and takes on a strong ecological posture in the studio. All the pieces are single-fired, cutting out the time and energy of bisque firing. The fuel is waste drainoil which we collect free of charge, 165 gallons in a trip, from the service stations in Elko. Kilns are built with only one layer of firebricks. The outside facing is laid up with earthen bricks, made by the students. Labor costs are not calculated. The cash saving is the margin we grow on.

These practices obviously help the school's finances. Equally important is what the students learn from this lean life-style. If they carry the patterns they have lived here into their own studios, their chances of survival as potters are increased.

Though my teaching of clay techniques and aesthetics would probably be better described by a former student, what I try to do is create an environment for learning—an adequate studio that is well-equipped but not lavish. I hope to remain a teacher who is committed to his personal vision first and works hard to materialize it, but still one who has the time and interest to answer questions. A teacher one uses like a reference book, pulled aside when there is no other way to solve a problem.

Here students have a block of time, a month or a year, that most have never had before. For the college students it is a break when there are no assignments; no history nor English papers to take them away from clay. For the production potters there are no urgent orders for planters, pitchers, and teapots; no one telling them what they *should* be doing. At its best this situation opens up a space where one can look deep and see what he or she *wants* to do.

Mostly I keep a low profile, but for continuity I still give a weekly critique, slide show, and demonstration. This is not intended to dominate nor fill the student with my philosophy, but is served up in the manner Hsiang Ju Lin describes hors d'oeuvres; they ". . . must taste clean. This means that their taste must be clear and definite, but not lingering. They must be like epigrams, pithy, amusing, light and brief."[1]

TECHNICAL INNOVATIONS?

It was the beginning of a particularly snowy winter when Fred Elliott, a neighbor on unemployment, asked me to teach him how to make flowerpots. By profession he is a core driller and by nature he thinks in mechanic-logic. Since I always have some machine around that needs repair, we traded skills: he fixed my cement mixer and I taught him how to throw pots.

By Christmas Fred had made, glazed, and fired flowerpots for all of his relatives. Before the ground had thawed enough for him to start drilling again, he had a knowledgeable foundation in ceramics—built by his inquisitive enthusiasm. Along with regular subscriptions to *Popular Mechanics, Popular Science,* and *Road & Track,* he now received *Ceramics*

4. Summer students rakuing, 1969. (*Larry Logan*)

5. Drainoil storage and preheating system. (*Ron Moroni*)

Monthly and *Studio Potter*. He read Leach, Cardew, Nelson, Olsen, and Yanagi, and had surfaced with this gnawing realization (one I always hope for in promising students) that, "Hey, my teacher hasn't been telling me everything!"

When I wandered into the Tavern one night, Fred called me over and started in, "I've been thinking. Those technical innovations you've put to work around the studio . . . they've come about only because you . . . because you're lazy, ignorant, and cheap." Fred is direct that way. He said it to me in the manner he might explain the principles of the internal-combustion engine—"compression, ignition, power, exhaust."

I did not agree right then. Fred had described my professional habits in terms I seldom used in reference to myself. But his tone was not pejorative. He spoke through a grin of discovery. The inspiration that had come was that his teacher: (1) stopped bisquing from laziness; (2) applied glaze to dry pots from ignorance of the leather-hard techniques; (3) and switched to drainoil for fuel because it was free. My immediate reply was, "Yes and no."

By now the time limit for a snappy comeback has lapsed. This book is a follow-up: a detailed account of what my student succinctly summarized. In describing techniques I will explain precisely, in detail, the steps I have taken to make wet glaze adhere to dry pots, the size of pipes I have wrenched together to make a burner fire, etc. These minutiae are important only as the focus for an isolated example. Do not confuse a personal preference, a regional prejudice, or a Rube Goldberg with spaceage technology.

Fred is no longer interested in making pots (he is now a drilling supervisor), so I am addressing this book to the students of ceramics, in school or out, middle-aged or young, who are intent on going through life with clay on their hands. You have learned to glaze bisqueware, fire with gas, and, if you have not yet helped construct a kiln, you have at least seen one being built. You are energetic, but short of cash, and always on the lookout for technical tidbits that will make studio life viable.

Everything outlined in this book works and, at the risk of appearing a little mechanically naïve, I have intentionally included a number of my false starts and dead ends. There is no reason another potter should make the same mistakes. Brand names of tools and machines are mentioned parenthetically as a starting point, not as an endorsement. If you cannot find a "Charles Heavy Fluid & Grease Pump" at your local auto parts store, devise another system. Ask the clerk for a substitute. Inquire politely at different service stations as to how they pump out their drainoil. If you do not have an 80-mesh screen for dusting ash on a pot, before you go and order one, try the screens you do have. The same goes for kilns. Many designs will work. The brand of insulation, shape of the arch, number of burner ports, fuel, blower, and chimney height are contingencies.

Root thinking is what I promote: a methodology that is long on principles, encourages substitution, and expects a variety of solutions to flower. This philosophy is nurtured by and finally becomes engrained in potters on a low budget. You thrive like a weed in any soil, in any climate, in good weather or bad.

STOPPING THE BISQUE

I learned to hate bisque firing early because, I think, I never really understood why all potters did it. My teacher said, "You bisque so that you can apply a glaze to your piece." This was never a wholly satisfactory answer, hence my poor attitude developed.

Opening a bisque kiln was not like Christmas. The burden of fetching and stacking the greenware, bricking in the door, and firing for hours was much the same as with a glaze kiln, but there was no joy for the potter—only a kiln full of dull, salmon-pink pots that needed glaze.

The cadence of sequential firing was strong in the late fifties (bisque, glaze, bisque, glaze, bisque . . .) when I marched into Beginning Ceramics 101. There were only a few textbooks in the field and their references to single-firing were not written to encourage the practice. They all sounded like this:

> A custom predating the bisque firing of greenware. Though there are obvious advantages, the drawbacks are numerous, *e.g.*, vessels are likely to crack or dissolve during glaze application; only a limited number of glazes fit, most of these being brown slip glazes of the Albany type; there is a high percentage of loss from accidents during firing.

My teacher had read the books.

Twenty years later there are more books and more potters, but very little single-firing going on. My theory is that it is because we are college-educated potters.

I studied first on campus with a teacher who learned in college from a teacher who had done the same. There may be nothing wrong with this system, but it breeds an inordinate respect for the Word, lectured or written.

I easily slipped into the habit of firing twice. Like any other tyranny I never felt a loss of freedom once I got into the practice. I accepted it. Bisquing became routine.

When I was in graduate school in the spring of 1965, I read every book in the Claremont College's library related to the history and practice of the ceramic arts. At that time it was not a difficult project. Today merely collecting a bibliography would be worth three credits. Part of my motive for doing research was to learn all I could about the historical technique of salt glazing. Several books mentioned in passing that traditional German and English salt-glazed pottery was only fired once. So naturally, as I began salt glazing, I began single-firing.

The authors did not say at what stage—wet, leather-hard or dry—glaze had been applied to the old vessels. I waited until I had thrown what looked like a kilnful. By then most of my pieces were bone-dry. I poured some standard bisque glazes on the inside of narrow-necked forms where I suspected no sodium would reach. On some I gave a little flourish of slip or sgraffito decoration to the outside. Sure enough a few pots cracked open and one or two glazes flaked off. But after several firings what I learned was liberating: (1) Raw glazing worked. Most pots do not crack when you wet them with glaze. In the kiln they matured and looked as good as twice-fired pots with half the work, or almost. (2) Glazes with a high-clay content adhered the best. (3) I liked the single-fire process. The immediacy. The intimacy of raw clay and glaze bond. The challenge of fragility. The finality of application with no erasures.

For the next two years all my clay work was raw-glazed and salt-fired (Plate 1). I was charmed with my new game. When I was hired for a college teaching position, the budget allowed only one kiln. I built a 65-cubic-foot cross-draft salt kiln and taught what I was excited about. Those students learned to fire once to cone 10 and then shovel salt. In retrospect I am embarrassed at having given them such a specialized view of ceramics, though a sprinkling of alumni later enrolled in graduate school and apparently quickly added the extra firing.

After those years of working exclusively with salt, I stopped. I was troubled by the surfaces on my pieces. None of the pots had any sizable area of bare clay with salt's classic orange-peel glaze, the unique quality that had originally attracted me. The latest work could have been divided into two piles—the pieces with bright, smooth glazes and those with leathery matt slips. I had lost the fascination for salt glazing. I could have produced the same range of surface textures in any stoneware kiln with less destructiveness to bricks and kiln furniture, and with no fumes.

That fall I resigned my teaching position and moved away from the salt kiln. I retreated to Tuscarora where I built an updraft for stoneware. I returned to the higher contrasts: the rough textures, the sharp definitions, the crisp outlines, the solid colors of regular, plain, unsalted stoneware. At the same time I was rekindling an old interest, I wanted to remain free of that ghost—the obligation to bisque.

While in that salt period, I concocted a white and a brown glaze that would mature without the flux of sodium fumes and used them on the protected interiors of casseroles and covered jars. Their reliability was security for me when I began raw glazing stoneware. More important at this transition was my confidence to relax and proceed joyfully doing something I had been soundly warned against.

I have since returned to salt but never exclusively: an off-and-on relationship best characterized as an affair with an ex-spouse—warm, appreciative, respectful, but with no thoughts of settling down again.

CHAPTER 2

Raw Glazing: Single-Firing, Once-Firing, Etc.

A BRIEF LOOK AT THE HISTORY OF GLAZING

Down through history potters are not remembered as writers, keeping diaries with glaze recipes and diagrams of their wheels. The great majority of them probably have been illiterate. Requisite knowledge of the craft was passed from mouth to ear, father to son, rather than through handbooks. There are sometimes census records or police blotters, but most of what I hear about these people and their ways of working come from the educated guess.

Discovering if a culture bisqued and when the practice began is aided by the archeologist who can make assumptions from evidence such as excavated bisque sherds at an ancient kiln site. From this kind of research I have learned that a complete history of single-firing would cover most of the history of glazed pottery. What I will attempt is to give a brief synopsis of the origins of bisque firing.

The simple diagram (Fig. 6) sent to me by a potter, David Cornell, gives an accurate outline of the story. Little more than the last 500 years,

```
first pot                                    1978
|---------------------------------|------------|
                         invention of bisque firing
```

6. "History of Ceramics."

out of 7,000 years of glazing, has been dominated by twice-firers. This is more explicit in a letter from an historian at the Victoria and Albert Museum, London: "Virtually the only types of ceramics that are not single-fired are, I suppose, most porcelains, creamware, and allied flint-bodied industrial wares including Staffordshire tortoiseshell ware of 'Whieldon' type, and tin-glazed wares (Maiolica, Delft, Faïence)."

Single-firing naturally preceded bisquing: normally potters do not do anything they do not have to do. Where, when, and why was the extra step introduced?

According to R. L. Hobson, "It was not the usual custom with Chinese Potters to harden the ware with a slight preliminary firing before proceeding to decorate and apply the glaze, and consequently such processes as underglaze painting in blue, embossing, etc., were undergone while the body was relatively soft and required exceedingly careful handling."[2] Ironically it was the impact of once-fired Chinese ceramics that started potters in other cultures bisquing.

It is documented in the eighth and ninth centuries T'ang Dynasty pottery (Plate 2) was exported to Mesopotamia where it was highly prized by the caliphs of Baghdad. Their domestic potters, attentive as all potters to the trends of the marketplace, were evidently quick to imitate. Lacking similar white clay they were forced to devise an alternative. How were they to make low-fire ochre-colored clay look like white clay?

At first they simply applied their regular clear glaze, decorated in pseudo-Chinese style and fired at a lower temperature. This resulted in an immature glaze, but one that was opaque and grayish white. Apparently this was not satisfactory, for soon they began covering the earthenware in a glaze opacified with tin.

The author and potter, Alan Caiger-Smith, wrote of the birth of bisquing: "There was a . . . difference between tin glazes and most transparent glazes. The latter could usually be applied to 'green', unfired vessels, so the pots were completed in a single firing. Tin glazes had to be applied to already fired or 'bisque' ware, partly because they had to form a thick coating and partly because they have a peculiar tendency to draw away from certain areas as they begin to melt, a characteristic known as 'crawling'. Therefore tin-glazed vessels had to be fired twice. . . ."[3] The Persians devised bisquing out of their frustrated attempts to copy raw-glazed whiteware.

From the Middle East the knowledge of tin-glazed, twice-fired earthenware spread. Islamic dominance, political and economic, of the Mediterranean was the carrier. Every culture that accepted the aesthetic of opaque decoration began bisquing out of necessity: Spanish lusterware, Italian maiolica, French faïence, and on into every country in Northern Europe.

By 1560, in the Netherlands, Dutch potters were using the glaze for its original purpose—their tin-glazed Delftware now imitated Chinese white porcelain. Less than a hundred years later in English Delftware, we find the British copying their neighbor's imitations.

In the mid-eighteenth century, with the rise of the Industrial Revolution, the practice of bisquing took on a broader importance. The potter Enoch Booth of Tunstall is credited with bringing bisquing to the great coal and clay center of Staffordshire. Bisqueware was less fragile than greenware which, as Hobson said, ". . . required exceedingly careful handling." The practice of bisquing was well-suited

7. Tin-glazed earthenware syrup jar; French, late sixteenth century. Height 8⅞ inches (19.8 cm.). Glaze was applied to bisqueware. (*Crown Copyright. Victoria and Albert Museum, London*)

8. Earthenware inkstand with loose drawer; Italian, seventeenth century. Height 10½ inches (26.7 cm.). Glaze was applied to bisqueware. (*Crown Copyright. Victoria and Albert Museum, London*)

to the growing factories with their division of labor, for it enabled the owners to exploit a larger number of semiskilled workers—landless farmers and their inattentive children.

Of course, all over the world some folk potters continued with the parallel tradition of single-firing. Enclaves of potters applying clear glaze to raw clay have survived in villages of Cornwall and hollows in Appalachia (Plates 3, 4, and 5). But it can be assumed that the mass of pottery since about 1500, admired, collected, and passed down to us, went through a kiln twice.

Summarizing from an historical perspective, bisque firing does show two specific advantages: Ware is less fragile when handled for decorating, and thick, opaque glazes can be applied safely and effectively. When these were not the overriding concerns, once-firing continued an unbroken tradition.

An anecdote came up when I visited China that made me believe the chain of bisque influence was complete. Our delegation toured the Shiwan Art Pottery in Fushan. That area has been prominent since the Sung Dynasty, the potters bending like the willow with the prevailing political tastes, but always producing a range of high- and low-fired ware from two local clays. The People's Republic emphasizes production of "artistic ceramics" to export in exchange for much-needed foreign currency.

Four chambers of their traditional climbing "Dragon Kiln" were loaded with raw-glazed figurines: Lu Hsun, Dr. Norman Bethune, heroic soldiers and happy peasants. The center chamber was filled with saggars enclosing the only bisqued ware: vases covered with a thick application of glaze. These would mature yellow, blue, and green with large, novelty crystals blossoming randomly on the surface—"a very popular glaze with foreigners," according to our official guide.

WHY GLAZE?

For me dropping the bisque step was like a Christian doubting the Virgin Birth: as soon as I removed the keystone of faith, the whole arch collapsed. I was forced to rethink the orthodoxy of glazing from the beginning. In this confusion, while rebuilding, I mulled over—"If bisquing is not always necessary, neither is glazing. What is a glaze, anyway? How do I want to make one? What ingredients do I prefer? When can I do without glaze? Does that piece need glaze? Does this one? What for?"

In the early sixties, the potter Valley Pousony suggested to The Kiln Club in Washington, D.C., that they sponsor a juried exhibition of bisque, undecorated vessels. I think her objective was to chastise potters who were steadily making weak shapes clothed in inappropriate and/or ostentatious glazes. What she suggested amounted to an outrageous ceramic equivalent of a Miss Nude America contest. The idea died not because she overstated her point, but because she was too close to being right.

9. Unglazed earthenware Cherokee Indian vessel; date unknown. Height 9½ inches (24.1 cm.). Author's collection. (*Valerie Parks*)

It is said that through the centuries glaze was applied to clay for motives both utilitarian and playful. The desire to make a vessel impervious to water and easy to clean is common and would account for a clear glaze on the inside of a bowl or the face of a platter. On the other hand, glaze on the outside of a pot is almost certainly in the realm of decoration: colors, textures, opacity, brushwork, sgraffito, slip-trailing. A case is made for the playful origins of decoration in a story related by Harry Davis in *Studio Potter*: "When Michael Cardew was in New Zealand, he showed us slides of Nigerian pots and remarked that the more primitive the tribe the more prone the people were to decorate their pots. Hearing this I was reminded of something which had greatly puzzled me when I was in West Africa 25 years ago. . . . I used to come upon . . . abandoned settlements which were always littered with pot sherds. The puzzling thing was that on these early sites the pots were mostly decorated, whereas, the contemporary pots were mostly plain, not that the contemporary ones were decadent, they were not; but as I now see it, this was simply evidence that the more primitive communities were more prone to play creatively, and had less of an eye on the market."[4]

He is speaking here of an isolated example, but two points come across with universality—decorating can be a primitive form of play, and the marketplace can seduce that child. In our culture there is more temptation to abuse our playfulness in overdecorating for the market—craft fair or exhibition—than underdecorating.

In the utilitarian context, glaze on a pot is a must, a social obligation, a sanitary expectation; but when you are decorating, the question to glaze, how much, or not to glaze, is private, very personal, and hopefully, still playful.

WHAT IS GLAZE?

Simply, glaze is a glass that adheres to clay. Ancient precedents abound. The earliest evidence of its use was that of the Egyptians in

10. Unglazed earthenware jug; French, fourteenth century. Height 6½ inches (16.5 cm.). (*Crown Copyright. Victoria and Albert Museum, London*)

5000 B.C., who rolled out beads of clay mixed with a sand high in sodium salts. Before the birth of Christ, Chou Dynasty potters were combining wood ash with feldspar and applying this to the surface of raw stoneware. In the eleventh century A.D., Germans stoked their kilns till the ware reached maturity, then threw in salt. The medieval English potter put galena ore in a rough cloth sack and dusted the fine powder on wet, freshly thrown jugs. All the early single-firing cultures had in common an empirical knowledge of the three ingredients required to form a glass skin on clay: (1) silica (the basis of any glass); (2) flux (to melt the silica); (3) alumina (for viscosity, to hold the glass on the clay). Bernard Leach refers anthropomorphically to these three as bones, blood, and flesh.

With Egyptian beads, silica came from both the clay and the sand; flux from the sodium in the sand; alumina from the clay. In the early Chinese glaze, silica was provided by the ash

11. Lion Rampant dish, earthenware, by Thomas Toft; English, late seventeenth century. Diameter 17½ inches (44.5 cm.). (*Crown Copyright. Victoria and Albert Museum, London*)

and feldspar; flux primarily by the ash; alumina by the feldspar. When the Germans salted a hot kiln, the clay surface of the pots surrendered the necessary alumina and the silica, which was fluxed by the action of the sodium vapors. Similarly, the medieval potter relied on the clay for silica and alumina, but in his case the flux was powdered lead.

Temperatures reached in these random kilns were both extremes: Egyptian paste and lead glaze below 1830° F. (1000° C.); celadons and salt-glazed stoneware above 2300° F. (1250° C.). The middle range was probably avoided because at very high and very low temperatures glaze composition requires fewer ingredients. Low temperature fluxes, such as borax, colemanite, or lead, will form rudimentary glazes when mixed with almost any silica-rich material at ratios of 1:1 or 2:1. In the high temperature range, few materials can resist melting. With little else added, earthenware clays become slip glazes, wood ashes flow into runny, semitransparent glazes, and impure feldspars mature as fat, opaque glazes.

THEORIES AND METHODS OF MAKING GLAZE

Only in the last century have we had a standard system for expressing glazes as formulae. This system is called the Unity Formula (also referred to as Seger Formula, Molecular Formula, Empirical Formula). It allows us to describe a glaze by the proportions of the constituent molecules. Ingredients are examined according to their function; their ratio as a group is then compared to the ideal ratio for a projected firing temperature. If a balance is achieved, the glaze recipe should work—though experiments still must be run.

This formula was devised originally by the German chemist, Hermann A. Seger (1839–94), the same scientist who introduced the first pyrometric cone for calibrating firing temperatures. Though the concept of developing glazes through chemistry is basic to today's ceramic industry and is taught in all college art-pottery classes, it has not caught on with all studio potters. The same goes for Mr. Seger's cone; there are still holdouts who mix a little clay with a little glaze and roll out their own crude cones, precisely gauged for personal needs.

Potters are at least as varied in their approach to life as any other cross section in the population, and their attitudes toward glaze reflect this. Some do follow science; others borrow recipes from magazines and books; or skip the exercise of weighing and measuring and purchase prepared glazes ("You don't look down on a painter who buys his colors in tubes instead of grinding his pigments." True); or put their faith in one of the many trial-and-error cults. A few examples follow.

There is an often retold story of how Peter Voulkos taught glaze calculation to students at the University of California-Berkeley. The students assembled in the materials room. The problem assigned was to invent their own cone 10 glaze. "Take a scoop of any three chemicals. Whatever looks good to you. Mix them with water and put it on a pot. If the first batch doesn't work, keep trying." The class was over. The story may not be true, but even as a persistent myth it brings attention to an experiential way to learn about glaze ingredients. Chemistry with its Unity Formula, molecular weights, and equivalents, is not the only path that leads through the mystery, just the most mathematical one.

If a student takes a pinch of every powdered ingredient in the glaze room and places each sample in a finger depression on a clay slab—after firing, the results will give back sufficient information about the fluxing value of each one to point in the direction of which ones to use in combination for a glaze.

After such an initial look at commercial glaze materials in the fired state, the next step is to become more knowledgeable by organizing and charting them according to their major function. Refer to a ceramic materials catalog or text to supplement the leads supplied by the firing. Though few chemicals are pure in function, *e.g.*, feldspar has some silica and flux in addition to alumina, general use helps separate them.

Silica (bones)	*Flux (blood)*	*Alumina (flesh)*
quartz	barium	kaolin
flint	boron	ball clay
sand	calcium	feldspar
	dolomite	
	lead	
	magnesium, etc.	

With only this minimal knowledge a glaze can be invented. Arbitrarily take the listing at the top of each column for a beginning. Establishing the proportion of each ingredient is the problem. Constructing a line or a triaxial blend are graphic methods. They can be used to better understand standard glaze materials or interesting unknowns (purple dirt, a white rock, a black clay) that you might stumble upon.

For a line blend (Fig. 12), roll out a slab of clay long enough and wide enough to allow you six thumb-sized depressions. Say I have a dirt sample that from a previous test firing I know melts too much. I try to stiffen it with additions of feldspar. After firing the line blend, I will have a range of four possibilities. Sometimes this is enough to make a glaze.

More often a glaze is a blend of at least three to five materials. For this reason a triaxial blend (Fig. 13) will give a better understanding of

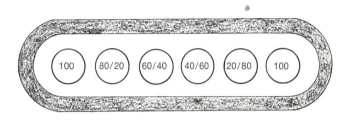

12. Line blend. (*Valerie Parks*)

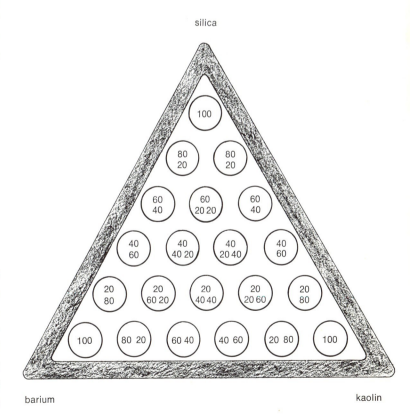

13. Triaxial blend. (*Valerie Parks*)

glazes and a more realistic look at the potential of a new material.

Roll out a slab of clay and inscribe an equilateral triangle and push thumb-sized indentations into the clay. At each point on the triangle the depressions hold 100 percent samples. Moving on a straight line from silica toward barium, at every depression 20 percent of the silica is replaced by an equivalent amount of barium. The amount of each material to be placed in the central depressions is again calculated by beginning at a corner and subtracting 20 percent for each position it is removed from that corner. Percentages can be taken by weight or measure, but for an accurate test it is good practice to blend thoroughly each sample with water before filling the indentation.

In this example the spots on the line between silica and kaolin could be disregarded since predictably no melting will occur. But if I substitute a less refractory clay for kaolin, say a local creek bed clay, this unknown mixture might include enough flux to mature with silica. The fired results of a triaxial typically present me with three to five glaze dots for interpretation. Depending partially on my expectations for color, opacity, and texture, I mix larger amounts of one or two of the most promising tests and apply them to individual pots, leaving the lower two-thirds bare clay for running room. From the next firing I have a broader view of the characteristics of these glazes, in particular whether or not they flaw in single-firing. Fine tuning of the recipe may be required: a slight increase in clay to counteract crawling or the addition of auxiliary fluxes.

I admit to being superstitious when it is time to test a new glaze on a pot. A promising sample comes out of the kiln. The logical next step is to mix up a larger batch and apply it to one of the rejected pieces that are always sitting around on the periphery of a glaze room. In recent years I have improved my degree of success by following the Incan example (the priests did not offer up the aged, malformed, and derelict)—I pick from my best, fresh, lively, well-thrown pieces. Consistently, risk and sacrifice generate the most exciting results.

The Canadian potter Robin Hopper wrote of an interesting system in *Ceramic Review* which he devised for teaching how to make glazes: "... I hate maths.... I found that most art students had an incredible inability to manage even fairly simple arithmetic; and that molecular theory, which is dependent on maths, was really out of the question to a great majority of people...." His scheme is predicated on the understanding that different fluxes cause metallic oxides to react in different ways, *i.e.*, barium makes iron fire blue or yellow, cobalt a bright blue, and copper blue-green; magnesium turns cobalt pink to purple; zinc mixed with iron gives mustard yellow.

He examined fifty cone 9 glazes and deleted the prime color-altering fluxes: ash, barium, colemanite, dolomite, frits, lithium, potassium, sodium, and zinc; and opacifiers such as opax, superpax, and zircopax. Then adding up and averaging the amounts of the remaining chemicals, he arrived at a skeletal recipe: feldspar 35; kaolin 12; ball clay 17; whiting 12; silica 7—for a total of 83. "If a glaze adds up to 100, calculating percentages of oxides is less demanding on the student. So to complete a glaze ... 17 of any one of the colour affecting fluxes is added. More than one can be added as long as the total amounts to 17." Though there were occasional failures in his class, the high success rate encouraged further experiments.

Material	Matt Variation Cones 8-10	Shiny Variation Cones 8-10	Variation for Cone 6 Shiny to Matt
feldspar (any)	35	35	35
kaolin (any)	12	—	—
ball clay (any)	17	17	12
whiting	12	12	17
flint	7	19	19
Total	83	83	83

Another unscientific glaze system comes from England and reportedly is popular even with mature artist-potters weak in math.

"4-3-2-1"

feldspar	4
silica	3
limestone	2
clay	1

According to Michael Cardew, "With reasonably normal materials this cannot fail to make a cone 8 glaze."[5] For application on an unfired pot, I recommend a plastic clay, E. P. Kaolin or ball clay.

RAW GLAZE VERSUS BISQUE GLAZE

The glaze recipes you see today posted on studio walls or listed in books and articles are calculated for application to bisqueware. When a new student confronts me with a superglaze recipe (from his last teacher's notebook), I say, "Try it." Many bisque glazes will single-fire on dry ware without a blemish. If one of them crawls, I suggest substituting ball clay for kaolin. If the recipe does not list kaolin, add between three and five percent bentonite.

Out of curiosity I ran tests with twelve cone 10 glaze samples from a commercial ceramic supply house: Tenmoku, Egg Shell Matt, Chün, Clear, etc. Arbitrarily I divided the bags into two piles. Three percent bentonite was added to half of the samples and five percent to the others. These glazes were mixed and poured on separate mugs—twelve leather-hard and twelve bone-dry. After firing, the results were:

Dry application—success, twelve; crawling, zero

Leather-hard application—success, three; crawling, nine

This outcome made me suspicious that on dry clay these glazes might work without bentonite, so I fired another twelve mugs with straight samples:

Success, nine; crawling, three

Regardless of the final score, it was not an unqualified endorsement for dry application. Physically the successful glazes were not flawed, but aesthetically they were not true to their labels, particularly the Chün and Tenmoku, which appeared flat and depthless. In contrast, on the leather-hard samples: Chün fired out opaque, opalescent, with a haunting pale blue cast; Tenmoku was a deep brown with rich rust and black spots.

The above problem, as well as other advantages and disadvantages for each system of raw glazing, will be discussed later in separate sections. For now there is one primary difference to remember—the potential for shrinkage still latent in the clay body at the moment of glaze application determines the plastic content needed in the glaze. A bisque pot has been preshrunk, therefore, little or no clay is necessary. A dry, unfired pot needs only enough clay in its glaze to compensate for the shrinkage during firing. Leather-hard or wet pieces require a very high-clay glaze that will shrink in unison with the body and stay adhered through both drying and firing.

THE RELATIONSHIP BETWEEN CLAY AND RAW GLAZE

The question comes up, "Did you have to change any forming or design techniques when you stopped bisquing?" My answer is, "No, I haven't." Of course, even when I was bisquing, my pottery seemed to express, for better or worse, something of a peasant touch—thick lips, solid necks, ample bodies, and wide, rough feet (right out of a Bruegel painting). Vessels like these are resilient and hard to crack.

Not everyone works my way. So in corresponding with other single-firing potters, I asked them the same question. A few responded hesitantly: "My only success has been with smaller things." "Thin pots are difficult to glaze." "Can't have overly thin bottoms." My favorite letters read like testimonials. From Tony Evans: "My work has changed considerably since I started to once-fire.... I have come to understand far more intimately the work of the country potter before the turn of the century (who nearly always once-fired). Many of the shapes he arrived at and decorations he used seem to be as a direct result of once-firing. My work often arrives at the same conclusions." Andrew Holden: "I think my pots are better-made these days, as raw glazing sorts out the over turned or poorly thrown." Sandra Johnstone: "The biggest change was [the] absolute necessity to construct pieces well—no flimsy handles, thick bottoms, or thin tops." But most potters replied to my question with a flat "No."

The clay body that you throw with does not necessarily have to change, either. The decision hinges on when you wish to apply glaze—when the clay is wet, leather-hard, or dry. With the first two the most frequent crisis happens when added moisture weakens a pot, causing it to slump or collapse. A tight, smooth, fine-particle, highly plastic clay body is less absorbent, and, therefore, recommended. For dry application the opposite properties are attributes—an open. grogged, less plastic mixture. When dry clay is moistened, it expands in proportion to its plasticity. If it swells too much, the walls crack.

So the choice is clear—pick the method that fits your present clay or change your clay to fit the method.

CHAPTER **3**

The Application and the Fire

APPLYING GLAZE TO BONE-DRY CLAY

I begin by describing applying glaze to bone-dry clay because it is the way I work. My faith in raw glazing was built with these techniques which developed from the onset when I innocently stopped bisquing (the idea never crossed my mind to attempt pouring a liquid glaze on a piece of clay that was still wet). Today I continue using the same method exclusively. Habit.

Other bone-dry glazers have shared their reasons with me. Jim Allen said: "I found a great difference between glazes that would work on leather-hard or wet ware, and glazes that worked on dry ware. I decided to glaze at dry since it eliminated many problems, such as trying to glaze when the pots are just right. Now, I throw a pot—set it on a shelf—come back to it when it's dry, and I can glaze it anytime thereafter." Peter Sohngen wrote very simply: "Bone-dry pots are easier to handle." Paul Soldner spoke up for decorative reasons: "I like the drier clay to keep edges sharper than soft (wet) clay. It's a matter of embellishment preference" (Plate 6).

Here at a high altitude, in a dry climate where there is seldom a rain all summer, maintaining any consistent level of moisture in a group of unglazed pots would be impossible short of building an airtight damproom. Certainly I could watch my pieces more closely as they dried, and then glaze singly when each was at the right moment of leather-hardness. This would demand from me an unappealing pattern of vigilance. Although I do not like to delay glazing until a potential kilnload of raw pots crowds the studio, waiting to be glazed, I cannot make myself set up and clean up a glaze table for just one or two pieces. I do my best decorating when I am faced with a group of related dry forms. Glazing a series of a dozen or more vessels seems to dissolve my self-consciousness, loosen my elbows and wrists, and helps reinforce a coherence in the group.

14. Stoneware plate by Peter Sohngen. 8 x 8 inches (20.3 x 20.3 cm.). Glaze was applied to dry clay. (*Peter Sohngen*)

15. "Raw-glazed ware waiting to go in kiln." Studio of Betty Woodman. (*Betty Woodman*)

Preparing to Glaze

Mixing glazes is a slow morning's work. Starting with five-gallon buckets filled one-third with water, weigh out the dry ingredients and dump them in—first the clay materials, then the heavy nonplastics on top to sink the lot. Resist that impulse to get right in stirring; instead, walk away for an hour or so to give all of the fine particles enough time to become waterlogged. Early agitation makes a lumpy glaze.

Though electric mixers on the market can be helpful, your hand should at least make a few slow passes to be certain the glaze is homogeneous in texture and color. Finally, pour it back and forth through a 30-mesh window screen until there is no material residue showing.

Glaze is applied more thinly to bone-dry clay than to leather-hard or bisque. If a piece is coated too thickly, the lip can dissolve, the wall may crack, or a handle fall off. Speed of application is one factor that determines how much glaze stays on a pot. But, accepting speed as a constant with each potter, the prime determinate is the consistency of the liquid. Our English language is short on precise terms to help us describe the subtleties. Potters use dairy similes—like yogurt; like thick cream; like half-and-half; like milk. "Half-and-half" is fluid enough for average bone-dry ware. With a hydrometer, the Specific Gravity reads between 1.35 and 1.4 for most, though I have a favorite glaze that is safely applied at 1.7. The perimeter is wide. When you are up to your elbow in a bucket, the feel comes quickly. I think of fresh goat's milk.

Next I add a large handful of dextrine to each bucket. This helps to keep the glaze ingredients in suspension, and will later strengthen the bond of glaze to clay—preventing scuffing, flaking, and the tendency to crawl. If a particular glaze has an inclination to settle rapidly, I stir in more dextrine. This being an organic starch by-product, it burns out early in the firing, and the amount has no effect on the glaze. A capful of Clorox thrown in the bucket will discourage the inevitable odors of fermentation.

Other binders can be ordered from ceramic supply catalogs (gum tragacanth, gum arabic, etc.), with instructions, or purchased off the shelves of your supermarket (corn syrup, molasses, cornstarch, and wheat paste—used in amounts of one percent or more). I have read where gelatin is suggested and, though I have never tried it, the vision of an overdose in a bucket scares me. The recommended procedure is to mix the powder 1:4 with water, and then add parts of this to your glaze on a ratio of no more than 1:6.

Dry pots are more fragile than bisqueware. You can prevent accidents in the glaze room by setting up carefully and prearranging the area to anticipate your desires. If you plan to use, say, two glazes in combination on a series of bowls—stir up *both glazes* in advance. If these bowls are large and you intend to pour over the outside of them, place an old refrigerator shelf-grill on top of an empty bucket. Position a separate cup for ladling next to each glaze bucket. Have all the tools you will need in reach. Do not get me wrong—raw glazing is not like a timed, cross-country race, rather, more of a methodical jog through familiar country but allowing no pauses nor detours.

Another essential is a handy bucket of clean water, with sponge. As soon as glaze is poured inside a bowl, as this liquid is sloshed around, the glaze water is absorbed and causes the interior surface of clay to expand. This is a natural reaction of bone-dry clay. Unless some form of compensating moisture is applied to the outside, the bowl is likely to crack. Of course, a coat of glaze will relieve the pressure, but, if the exterior is to be left unglazed, a quick dip in water, a spray, or a light sponging compensates.

A story may help dramatize the point. Potter-sculptor Joe Soldate drove up one summer from Los Angeles to Tuscarora to work awhile in the studio. He came as an old friend, not a new student—so I left him on his own and forgot that he was unaccustomed to raw glazing.

One afternoon Joe set out six pitchers for glazing. He stirred up a glossy oatmeal glaze and poured it in and out of each. When he set the last pitcher down, he looked around to locate the bucket with matt green which he envisioned using on the outside. By the time he stirred it, squeezed the lumps out, and washed and dried his hands, he was ready to continue glazing. Facing him now were twelve half-pitchers. The punishment was swift and the lesson clear. Dry greenware is delicate and fragile; whether these qualities bring disaster or whether they can give immediacy and dignity to vessels depends mostly on how long a potter has been raw glazing. Joe laughed.

A final precaution. Have your pottery completely dry before any glaze goes on. If no moisture difference is visible, between top and bottom, it is safe to proceed. On the other hand, if the foot is still darker than the lip, and a glaze is applied, a horizontal, hairline crack will appear on the border of the moist area. What has happened is that the drier clay absorbed more glaze water and consequently its rate of expansion was greater.

Once clay has dried completely there is no time limit on its shelf life: a dry pot can be glazed today or next year. Accumulating dust and fingerprints, which cause glazes to crawl on bisqueware, never seem to trouble dry pots. Half the time I blow the dust off, but never thoroughly.

There are no new techniques for applying a glaze to an unfired vessel; the ones described here should be familiar from bisque-firing days —pouring, dipping, brushing, spraying, and dusting. I review them only to emphasize the minor, though important, variations in timing and care; to suggest remedies for directly related problems; and, of course, to encourage more potters to stop bisquing.

Before glazes are put on, compatible slips or oxide mixtures can be applied, but unlike on bisque, if a mistake is made or a second thought comes up, your dry clay cannot be taken to the sink and have its glazes washed off. The requisite scrubbing with a wet sponge, or even dry steel wool, will sadly deteriorate the surface and can threaten the life of a piece. There is no erasing. Think, do it, and fire. This limitation need not be considered negatively as it can build character. The absence of a second chance, at best, cements a decisiveness and tension to once-fired clay.

Pouring and Dipping

The bulk of my studio pottery is decorated by pouring glaze inside and pouring or dipping the outside. Different shapes require slightly different handling, but there is a basic pattern:

—Fill a pot at least one-third full of glaze before swirling and pouring the liquid out (Fig. 16). A second filling, to cover an area you missed, can crack a thin clay wall.

—Now, without rush or delay, glaze the outside (Figs. 17, 18). If it is to be dipped, do this as soon as the interior glaze has lost its wet sheen.

—For pouring the outside of forms too large to hold, place a grill on top of the bucket where the pot will be inverted. The more familiar arrangement with the lip of a large pot resting on two sticks will not distribute weight to enough points, *i.e.*, the lip, softened by glaze, may dissolve and be scarred at the four points where it is in contact with the sticks.

—As soon as glaze ceases dripping, lift the piece, set it right side up, and check and repair any minor damage to glaze on the lip.

—Avoid handling the piece until it is again dry.

Flatware, plates, and platters have special problems getting through any kiln firing. Most pots that crack do so in the bottom and since plates are 90 percent bottom, they are often looked on as troublesome. I never glaze the outside of these shapes so I make certain that the unglazed area is moistened, either before or immediately after pouring glaze on the inside.

16. Author glazing inside of dry bowl. (*Valerie Parks*)

17. Author glazing outside of dry bowl. (*Valerie Parks*)

18. Author glazing outside of dry bowl. Note convenience of large foot. (*Valerie Parks*)

19. Brushing wax-resist emulsion to rim of platter. Moisture from the emulsion remains in the lip for up to eight hours. Glazing should take place within this time. (*Ron Moroni*)

20. Pouring glaze in dry platter. (*Ron Moroni*)

21. Pouring glaze out of dry platter. (*Ron Moroni*)

22. Sponging outside of platter with water to compensate for interior glaze-induced expansion. (*Ron Moroni*)

23. Turning freshly glazed platter sandwiched between two wooden bats to avoid stress. (*Ron Moroni*)

24. Chinese workers brushing glaze on dry figurines. Shiwan Pottery, Fushan, The People's Republic of China.

25. Train scene, low-fire. Height 7 inches (17.7 cm.). Glaze brushed on dry clay. Shiwan Pottery, Fushan, The People's Republic of China.

Brushing

I received a letter from Olin Russum explaining why and how he brushes glaze on raw clay: "Much of my work is large—imagine bisque firing 500 to 600 tiles and then glaze firing, my aching back, with some of the large tiles weighing 50 to 100 pounds. For the most part I brush glaze—although I do pour glazes for certain results. A scrub coat first on bone-dry ware. Then a second scuff coat, and for matt glazes a third coat. Very thick allover applications are impossible; but then I have no interest in this type of heavy obliteration of the texture and form. I do draw with glazes on top of a smooth coat, and this can often be ⅛ to ¼ inch thick and holds."

A complaint about brushing is that on certain clays the porosity of the body immediately sucks the water from the brush and restricts your movement to very short strokes. This can be overcome by putting on an initial "scrub coat" of dextrine and water, or diluted gelatin, to fill the pores. Then longer, freer, flowing brush-loads are possible.

Spraying

"I apply the glaze by spraying on either one or both sides (it doesn't seem to make much difference in what order or when), but the clay must be bone-dry," writes Bennett Bean. He further embellishes the surface while spraying by holding neoprene stencils that mask out and define areas of decoration.

Spraying is a sensible technique on dry clay. A mist of glaze settling on the surface certainly implants less water than any fluid application, consequently the pot undergoes less stress. The initial expense for equipment and its maintenance is a drawback.

Like the differences between a commercial spray-painted car and backyard hand-painted job, there is a message in the method you choose. The best results come from matching the technique with your aesthetics, rather than vice versa.

Dusting

Dusting is a technique as natural as gravity—one that puts no stress on clay and needs no expensive equipment. In Western culture its lineage goes back to medieval potters shaking cloth sacks filled with galena, the powdered lead ore drifting down and settling on fresh ware. (In fact the pots were not always still wet from throwing. There is evidence of dry pots being covered with slip or wheat paste just prior to dusting.) I have never dusted lead because of its toxic side effects, but do use the technique of sifting on various ashes (sagebrush, lemon wood, eucalyptus, trash, mixed hardwood, aspen, and chokecherry), dirt, Portland cement, and dry glaze mixes. A 60-mesh screen is my tool, and for protection I try to remember to wear a lightweight mask.

In Tuscarora, sage ash is a popular raw material because it is plentiful, easy to use, and melts into a serviceable glaze. At the turn of the century when the mines were active, sagebrush was the only fuel available to fire the mills. By the foundation of every mill site lies a pile of tons of pure, free ash. This is the only ash I have experience with that, with no additives, at cone 10 melts to a stiff, bright, utilitarian glaze: predominantly green, with yellow and brown areas (depending on thickness) and occasional streaks of blue.

The color, texture, and viscosity of any dusting material is determined by many variables—the clay body host and the thickness of application as well as its origin and composition. As always, experimentation is the only way to establish your point of reference.

For application I use the two basic methods: dry dusting and wet dusting. Both rely on a sieve as the tool, gravity for direction, surface angle and/or surface viscosity for thickness. Dry dusting is the sieving of a powder directly on a dry clay surface. The shape of the host determines the amount of glaze that will adhere. Flatware, broad-shouldered vessels, and pots with handles, spouts, or lids, are most receptive.

26. Low-fire plate, by Bennett Bean. Diameter 12 inches (30.4 cm.). Glaze sprayed on dry clay. (*Bennett Bean*)

27. Red earthenware jug; English, fifteenth century. Galena dusted onto wet slip. (*Crown Copyright. Victoria and Albert Museum, London*)

28. Dusting sagebrush ash on hanging planter. (*Valerie Parks*)

With wet dusting the shape is no limitation. This variation takes advantage of that temporary stickiness of a shiny wet glaze. Immediately after applying the liquid, sift on the dust. This allows dusting of sides, bellies, whatever, depending entirely on how the piece is held or turned. Wet dusting increases the number of glaze possibilities in geometric proportion to the number of dusts and liquid glazes on hand. For example, I have three shop glazes and four dusts that mature alone (on dry) or in combination (on wet). For a start this gives me seven basic glazes and twelve variations from which to choose.

A coat of wet slip or an organic binder can be used in place of liquid glaze. A binder such as dextrine or wheat paste, in thick solution, has the advantage of staying moist longer than slip or glaze.

Before firing, the surface of a dusted vessel is similar in appearance to a sprayed glaze: it is powdery and fragile. Damage can come not only from careless handling but also from curious insects and foul weather. I try to delay my dusting until the night before loading the kiln to limit the time spiders and flies have for crawling. A high wind on the loading day can unglaze everything.

29. Hanging planter after firing.

Tales of Woe: The Aggravations, Disadvantages, Problems—and the Cures

I have never heard a single-fire scare story that did not have truth in the plot. "Your pieces will crack." "Crumble." "Dissolve." "Glazes don't fit." "Flaking." "Crawling." "Beading." Etc. I have listened to quite a few. If you put them all together, there is consistency: they are told by honest people with little experience in firing only once; they are exaggerated; they justify the practice of twice-firing. Still there is truth here.

Regardless of the number of firings clay is put through, sometimes some pots crack or bloat and the glazes may crawl or pinhole. In the majority of cases you can isolate the cause and correct it, either scientifically or intuitively. Following is a checklist of major flaws that might be triggered by putting glaze on raw, dry clay together with suggested remedies.

PROBLEMS WITH CLAY

Cracking The only cure for cracking is prevention. As mentioned earlier, the expansion which takes place in clay when the inside glaze is applied must be equalized on the outside with an application of either glaze or water. Even after this precaution is taken, an S-crack may appear. If it opens up within moments after glaze application, this could be a sign the glaze went on too thickly. More water added to the glaze bucket should save the next piece.

Occasionally a favorite glaze will not take thinning without aesthetically altering its fired characteristics. When this is the case, preheat your ware on top of a heater or in an oven until it is as hot as you can handle. Pour the glaze in and out. The glaze water will evaporate so quickly that the clay will not have time to expand destructively. This hot-pot technique can be slow and awkward (painful). I have seldom had need to resort to it, but there are a few potters who prefer the insurance, and routinely heat all their platters over 18 inches before glazing. The final straw may be the reality that in single-firing the total fired-shrinkage of a piece is accomplished in only one setting. Poorly cleaned kiln shelves with spots of glaze, or a rough coat of kiln wash can impede the even movement of the base as it decreases in diameter. To facilitate the shrinking during firing, I dust a thin coat of alumina on the kiln shelves where wide or heavy pieces are to rest.

The blame for rim cracks is hard to place on the raw glazing technique. Whether in evidence as the work dries, after glaze application, or when unloading the kiln, the problem usually can be traced to throwing habits. These cracks are prevented if the lip is firmly compressed at intervals during the throwing and after any widening of the lip diameter. Some other possible causes with obvious remedies are: off-center throwing that results in grossly uneven walls; pushing too hard against the lip when anchoring a piece to be trimmed; rough handling at any stage prior to firing.

I pass on two general crack remedies which I have never tried, but were given to me by reliable potters. Spray your glazes if the shape of the piece allows, or pour glaze on the inside of a pot when it is leather-hard and on the outside when it is bone-dry. Tension can be avoided.

The composition of your clay body may be the villain. An extemely plastic clay, say one high in ball clay, will expand and contract during glazing in proportion to its usual shrinkage. Less stress is experienced by a clay body that: (1) includes ten percent or more nonplastic, grog, sand, or mica; (2) includes a large amount of kaolin, 30 to 50 percent; (3) excludes highly refined air-floated clay.

David Cornell sent me a suggested cure for the body that cracks from glaze application, but one in which you do not want to change any ingredients. The treatment is to adjust the pH (acidity/alkalinity) of your clay—the closer a clay's pH is to neutral, the denser and more impervious to water it will be. Industrial tests have shown that neutral, dry ware can be immersed in water for up to ten minutes without disintegrating. Add soda ash to neutralize an acidic clay or vinegar to an alkaline clay. An inexpensive soil-testing kit purchased from a nursery will test how your clay rates.

Clay body and pH factor adjustments should be saved for the last line of defense since most clays are not temperamental and accept a coat of glaze quite passively.

Handling Handling has to be the number one disparagement in textbook references to raw glazing. Unfired clay *is* quite fragile. Yes, the novice will see himself at least once holding a handle with the mug on the floor or wearing a casserole like a loose bracelet down around the elbow. But in retrospect it becomes self-evident that losses caused by mishandling can be avoided with common sense and practice.

Bloating Bloats are the result of gases forming and becoming sealed inside the clay wall. The gas is trapped because the surface of the clay vitrifies prematurely, due either to the early melting of applied glaze or the fluxing action of fuel vapors. In most cases the bloating gas is a by-product of unburned carbon. When it is denied access to atmospheric oxygen, it will rob what it can from iron oxide in the clay. The origin of this unwanted carbon may be organic matter in the body or excessive fuel in the early stages of firing.

Single-fired clay is prone to bloating. In a bisque kiln loaded with unglazed pieces, gases can readily escape through the porous clay walls. On the contrary, a pot being single-fired has its pores plugged with glaze, so it must be fired a little longer and slower through the early firing stages.

A bloat-like phenomenon unrelated to carbon, but just as annoying, can occur right after glaze is applied. Thin pots are highly susceptible. A blister forms from the approximate center in the clay wall cracking the moist, freshly glazed surface. It may expand inside and out.

Typically the drama begins like this: A glaze is poured into a bowl, then out. Directly the bowl is dipped (or the glaze poured) to coat the exterior. As the water is absorbed, the surface changes from shiny wet to dull matt—then the blister pops up, visibly and audibly. This is not the result of interior gaseous pressure, but the release of tensions created by dual, competitive expansion of the interior and exterior surfaces.

The easiest remedy for the piece in hand is to apply gentle fingertip pressure, inside and out, and pinch the blister flat. Because the clay is moist, it reunites and adheres nine times out of ten with no scar. To prevent these from forming on subsequent pieces, the glaze should be thinned. Another trick that works is to delay slightly the application of glaze to the outside.

PROBLEMS WITH THE GLAZE SURFACE

Most aggravations that spring up on the glaze surface have roots in the compatibility of clay body and glaze—evidence of a poor bond. The solutions I suggest deal only with changes in or additions to the glaze. I have always been hesitant to divorce myself from a faithful clay body, at least not from desire for a new glaze. Any number of different glazes satisfy the need, while an old familiar clay is sentimental.

Flaking Flaking refers to glazes that do not adhere well on application. When the glaze dries, it chips, cracks, peels, and drops off before the pot reaches the kiln. You seldom encounter this flaw except with new, untested glazes.

If a glaze flakes while you are handling the pot, the remedy may be simply to add a binder; three percent is a good starting point.

You may notice a dry glaze flaking before it has even been touched. If so, more binder should be the first treatment. Unfortunately, in most cases this is a symptom of unequal shrinkage, a serious incompatibility between clay and glaze. Either the glaze is too plastic or not plastic enough, usually the latter. If a widespread network of hairline cracks develops as the glaze dries, decrease the clay content and/or substitute less plastic clays in the recipe (*e.g.*, kaolin for ball clay).

The more common pattern that forms is composed of two or three vertical surface cracks. If you gently tap between them, a small, dried, irregularly shaped section of glaze drops off. What has happened is that the body shrank more than the glaze. The cure is an addition of three to five percent bentonite and/or the substitution of more plastic clay in the glaze (*e.g.*, ball clay for kaolin).

Lifting Lifting may develop after applying overlapping glazes to raw clay. The last coat of glaze peels loose from the first, or attaches tightly to it and lifts the first layer free of the clay. If fired, the glaze will crawl severely. There are four cures to be attempted singly or in combination: (1) apply overlapping glazes that are similar in the proportion of basic ingredients; (2) add more binder or bentonite to both glazes; (3) brush a thin scrub coat of binder on the clay prior to glazing; (4) apply the second glaze quickly, before the first has dried matt.

Circumventing a problem is also a solution. In order to achieve the effect of overlapping glazes, the shades of color, and the illusion of depth, I apply slips and oxides when my clay is leather-hard. Once a piece is dry I put on a single, overall glaze with no troubles.

Potters who raw glaze wet or leather-hard report routine success with overlapping. It may be true that your preferences in decorative techniques should help determine at what stage you apply glaze.

Crawling Crawling is a firing defect where the glaze splits open, rolls back on itself, and reveals the clay body. Glazes you use regularly seldom crawl. When they do, it is seen at the lip and is brought on by too thick an application. Easy to remedy. When a new glaze crawls, other than at the lip, this is sufficient evidence that the recipe needs altering. Again the familiar prescription is: substitute ball clay for kaolin and/or add three to five percent bentonite.

Blistering, Dunting, Pinholing, and Shivering From my experience and correspondence with dozens of potters who glaze raw, there seems to be no evidence or rumors that the causes of blistering, dunting, pinholing, and shivering are in any way related to not bisquing.

APPENDIX TO PROBLEMS IN GENERAL

Nothing happens always. There was a student who studied with me who definitely fell into the category one terse former art professor referred to as "manual idiots." This student read *The Odyssey* in Greek and Dostoevski in

30. Carp vase, by Frank Boyden; low-fire native Oregon clay and weathered beach sand. Height 16¾ inches (42.5 cm.). Glaze was applied to dry clay. (*Frank Boyden*)

32. Stoneware plate, by David Cornell. 12 x 12 inches (30.5 x 30.5 cm.). Glaze was applied to dry clay. (*David Cornell*)

OPPOSITE
31. Italian earthenware vase, by Betty Woodman. Height 10 inches (25.4 cm.). White slip brushed on wet pot, then lead-glazed when bone-dry. 1973. (*Betty Woodman*)

33. Stoneware covered jar, by Steven Hill. Height 14 inches (35.6 cm.). Glaze was applied to dry clay. (*Steven Hill*)

34. Porcelain bottle with crystalline glaze, by Phyllis Ihrman. Height 5 inches (12.7 cm.). Glaze was applied to leather-hard clay. (*Phyllis Ihrman*)

Russian. He eagerly watched my demonstrations, following them with hours of quiet practice in the studio. Still my messages never reached his fingertips. Sitting at the kick wheel, he used his hands like a sea lion would learning how to throw with flippers. In one push he could mash out a plate; a single mush formed a bowl. His glazing techniques closely paralleled his throwing.

That semester all of his ware was fired without a crack or a glaze blemish. Of course he had not understood my coaching on the absolute necessity of compressing clay, and on the tender delicacy of glazing dry, raw pottery. Since he left here, I have learned to qualify my technical dicta and I have composed a prologue for new students: "Pots are quick to make. Unfired clay can be recycled. Let precautions follow error. Don't take advice until you have made the same mistake twice."

APPLYING GLAZE TO WET AND LEATHER-HARD CLAY

I continue to glaze my work dry. My experience with damp pieces comes from playfully experimenting to understand the hows and whys. My knowledge and respect have grown through correspondence with persuasive studio potters who regularly glaze their ware before it dries. Phyllis Ihrman was particularly generous in sharing her manuscripts and articles with me. She began glazing as a student at the Detroit Society of Arts and Crafts, working under Professor John A. Foster. He stands out as a lonely teacher in the twentieth century; while bisquing prevailed all around him, he continued to instruct his students how to glaze leather-hard.

I can see clear advantages, especially at a lower altitude in a more humid climate where pots dry slowly. Less time elapses between giving birth to a vessel and dressing it up. Clay that has not lost all plasticity is more lively. Rather than having glaze be a glass skin on top of clay, the surface can develop as an impasto of the two. On a practical level, these glazes can be applied as thick as or thicker than bisque glazes without crawling or threatening the clay's integrity.

Clay-Glaze Balance

When glaze is applied to an object that is still plastic, or almost so, there needs to be a prerequisite shift in your attitude toward clay and your behavior with it. In contrast to the expansion caused by applying glaze to bone-dry pots, the response of damp clay is mild. At leather-hardness a pot has done so little shrinking that the absorption of liquid into the surface and the resulting expansion is minimal. Application can be more relaxed. The glaze and clay dry slowly together, shrinking in unison.

Typically the clay bodies are tight, smooth, and plastic; some include as much as 50 percent ball clay. High total shrinkage can be tolerated under these circumstances. An open clay is more likely to absorb water and weaken, sometimes requiring an overnight wait between glazing of the inside and the out. Without the pause, the clay regresses to an earlier state of moist, plastic delicacy, this being a nice way of saying that your favorite piece may distort or collapse. Handles and spouts may disunite and slide off.

These are reasons enough why, with a new technique, you should advance cautiously. Begin glazing small, uncomplicated pots until you progressively develop sensitivity to the nuances.

Because glazes must shrink in a one-to-one relationship with the body, very few glazes designated for bisqueware will fit. They were formulated with low plasticity anticipating application to preshrunk clay. In tests I ran with the twelve commercial glaze mixtures, nine crawled after I applied them to leather-hard pots.

Glazes

To establish parallel clay glaze shrinkage, there are several current theories, all similar in that each attacks the potential disharmony by raising the plasticity of the glaze. Peter Dick prescribes the simplest: "Just add six percent bentonite to a normal bisque glaze." A possible refinement on this comes from Carl Judson who believes that each glaze should contain the plastic equivalent of 40 to 50 percent ball clay. As an alternate to increasing the ball clay, he says eight to thirteen percent bentonite can be added to the recipe in place of all or part of the kaolin.

A system Bill Creitz relies on is quite similar, but with an interesting quirk—the substitution of a percentage of bentonite in place of feldspar. "Any glaze can be adjusted with a combination of ball clay and bentonite—twelve percent of each or more ball and less bentonite. Substitute bentonite for spar—the chemical formulas are quite close. With this basic method any glaze formula with twelve percent clay is easily converted to S[ingle]. F[ire]. A typical conversion with the 'Rhodes 32' or 'Mamo' glaze is as follows:

spar	5.0	4.3
ball clay	2.5	2.5
dolomite	2.0	2.0
whiting	.5	.5
zinc	.8	.8
bentonite	—	.7

In this conversion seven percent bentonite was substituted for spar. For more shrinkage, use more bentonite."

35. Bowls, by Peter Dick. Diameter 5 inches (12.7 cm.). Glaze was applied to leather-hard clay.

Two leather-hard glazers sent in suggestions that are applicable for those who prefer mixing glazes from native materials. Suzi Curtis offers a universal starting point: ". . . take five parts of clay and then . . . make it up to ten with three flux-like materials."

In contrast to her is Max Braverman, who is geographically very specific, though I suspect his methodology could be overlaid on other areas.

Favorite Recipe c[ones] 9–10:
1. Go to New Mexico.
2. Dig up some "dirt."
3. Put through same screen you use for preparing sand for plastering.
4. Store until ready to use.
5. Mix with water. (Minimum)
6. Put through 30-mesh screen.
7. Put through 50-mesh screen.
8. Pour and dip on pot as soft as can be handled.
9. Set aside and don't touch until leather-hard.

If glaze doesn't vitrify or is rough, 4a. Mix with unwashed screened fireplace ashes at about 1 ash to 3 dirt. (Wear gloves)

Result: Everything from grass green, deep green, brown, chocolate brown, brown-black, depending on the local clay and the degree of reduction.

Since all potters have favorite glaze recipes, those who convert to single-firing usually adjust with one or the other of the bentonite systems.

Warnings must accompany the use of bentonite, an extremely plastic volcanic clay. In water it swells twenty to thirty times the dry volume. (1) Never add it dry to a liquid glaze. Lumps will form and remain floating on the surface, insoluble for the near future. Instead, premix all ingredients dry, then add to water. (2) These glazes may have the thixotropic characteristic whereby they thicken at rest, becoming almost gelatinous, but when stirred they again liquify. Always agitate first. Then check the viscosity before adding more water. (3) Additional suspension agents or binders are unnecessary.

Application

Ordinarily a glaze for leather-hard application can be put on clay that is wet, soft leather, or leather-hard. But certain glazes, such as Braverman's, come proscribed to a particular dampness. To help describe these degrees of moisture, Phyllis Ihrman has defined a basic nomenclature:

wet	sticky
soft leather	trimmings come off in curls
leather-hard	trimmings come off in chips

A piece at either of the last two stages will be slightly inconsistent in moisture content from top to bottom. For example, the lip and handle of a pitcher will be the first areas to stiffen. They should be equalized by a quick dip in water, a spray, or a light sponging to control the glaze's tendency to flake and crawl. This remoistening can only be a touch-up job, never an attempt to reverse bone-dryness. Pots that have begun to change color will later require either a dry-application glaze or a bisque firing. Due to this problem, it is not uncommon for glazers of leather-hard ware to twice-fire a small percentage of their work.

POURING AND DIPPING

Glaze can be poured on the inside of a damp pot before it is trimmed—anytime after the clay is firm enough to handle. A teapot, for example, is thrown and set aside to stiffen. Next the inside is glazed, the foot trimmed, strainer holes carved, and finally the spout and handle attached. The pot is covered with a plastic sheet until all its parts have equalized in moisture. Then, or anytime thereafter (soft leather, leather-hard, or dry), the outside of the teapot is ready to glaze. As a general rule, the wetter the clay body, the thicker the liquid glaze can be. One potter who glazes wet pots describes the process as being "like brushing on yogurt."

BRUSHING

Compared to working on bone-dry clay, brushing glaze onto damp pottery is an effort-

36. "Round Black Set," jug, vase, and dish, by Andrew Lord. Earthenware. 1978. Jug size 9½ x 8 x 4 inches (24 x 20 x 11 cm.). Metallic black slip. (*B. van de Wetering*)

37. Peter Dick glazing leather-hard teapots and attaching spouts.

38. Five-gallon planters, by Larry Shep from the catalog of Shep Stoneware. Glaze was brushed on wet clay. (*Larry Shep*)

less, fluid act. At any of the three stages it is possible to lay down long, full strokes—in painterly style or simply as the means of covering a vessel from lip to foot. The thickness of the coat can be controlled easily and quickly varied. Massive pots that are too heavy to handle, or delicately thin ware which might turn limp if poured or dipped with glaze—these can safely be brushed.

A variation on brushing is practiced by Larry Shep on his large production ware. While a piece is still on the wheel, he squeezes out thick glaze with a syringe, then he smooths down the wet ridge using a flexible rubber rib or the palm of his hand and his fingers. Beside his wheel he keeps a dry glaze mix in a sieve. In his own words: "The reason for applying powdered glaze (mainly on the inside of open forms or bowls) is to dry the applied slip glaze somewhat so that the clay of the pot does not soak up too much added moisture of the glaze and weaken and collapse. Also, it speeds up the drying of the bottom which is a slower drying area."

SPRAYING

Spraying is another option for pieces that are hard to handle. Because of the low porosity of damp clay, the glaze should be prepared as thick as the nozzle of the spray gun will allow. For the same reason, you will need to spray on successive layers, with time between each to allow the wet surface to lose its shine.

SGRAFFITO DECORATION

Historically the temptation to scratch through a slip into leather-hard clay came to pottery long before glaze. When first a slip was applied that contrasted in color, the urge must have come to mind to pick up a stick, or fragment of bone, and scratch through.

The carving out of lines in leather-hard slip, and later in glaze, is a technique that can be executed swiftly or meticulously. The resulting contrast may be sharp or subtle. Refer to Chinese examples from the late T'ang and the Sung dynasties. Ceramic pillows from the Mi-hsien kilns in eastern Honan were made of a buff clay, then covered with white slip which was scratched in to portray detailed landscapes. The later Tz'u-chou ware, produced at kilns in the northeast, was out of light-colored clay, dipped in a brown glaze, and then areas were carved away.

Dry or bisqueware can be decorated by sgraffito, but their stiffness restricts the depth you can carve. Because of their porosity, whatever is applied to the surface dries quickly and is prone to chipping. Leather-hard clay is to sgraffito what bisque is to tin-glazing.

FIRING ONLY ONCE

Before loading a kiln the raw ware should be as air-dried as your climate allows. Since I glaze bone-dry, I apply glaze one day in anticipation of firing the next; in Tuscarora overnight is sufficient. Of course, there is no compulsion to fire the following day because greenware, glazed or unglazed, can sit around indefinitely.

I have been told that the single-firing stoneware kiln can be packed so tightly that pieces gently touch one another. It sounds plausible since the total fired shrinkage of pieces takes place in a single sitting; pots will shrink free of each other before the temperature is high enough for glazes to begin melting. Earthenware contracts less and, therefore, may require a separation between pieces. In practice I still cautiously leave about a 1/16-inch clearance between all pots in any firing.

In high fire, the drastic movement caused by shrinkage may produce a crack in the base of a pot if the piece is restrained by uneven kiln wash, glaze spots on the kiln shelf, or by its own rough surface. Flatware, plates, and platters, and any heavy object with a wide foot are susceptible. To facilitate a smooth, unobstructed diameter shrinkage, I dust a light coat of alumina on the plate shelves. These particles function like thousands of minute ball bearings. I try to be careful that none of the powder sifts down between shelves and onto the pots below; excess alumina on top of a bright glaze gives the surface the tactile quality of fine sandpaper. I recommend dusting the shelf outside the kiln and downwind from the door.

Alumina is also handy to prevent the sand and iron in your clay body from sticking lids to lips. Mix a large pinch with a little wax resist and brush this on both parts where they will be touching. The wax burns off early in the firing and leaves in place a fine protective coating of alumina. After unloading the kiln, the lids are loose, and the powder easily rubs off.

Start a single-firing like a bisque: candle and

39. Chinese pillow with sgraffito decoration; Sung Dynasty. Height 4 inches (10.2 cm.). Art and History Museum, Shanghai, The People's Republic of China.

proceed slowly to evaporate remaining moisture. If this warm-up is too rapid, pots explode. Then there is no choice but to cease firing. Unload the entire kiln, clean the debris out of the remaining pots, reload, and start again. Though such an accident is always disheartening, if it happens in a bisque kiln, it does not interrupt your firing schedule. In a single-fire, all those random crumbs and sherds, unless removed before glaze begins melting, will be glazed forever to the survivors.

As the kiln reaches red heat the schedule accelerates to the speed of a glaze firing. Between 1292° F. (700° C.) and 1832° F. (1000° C.) be certain the flame is burning clean. This facilitates complete combustion of all organic matter native to the clay as well as any soot that might have impregnated the body during firing. An hour of clear oxidation beginning at 1750° F. (950° C.) is an alternate solution. If pockets of carbon are not burned out prior to the clay's vitrification, the gases created will be unable to escape and will balloon as trapped pressure forms bloats.

The majority of my single-firing correspondents, wet and dry glazers, are in agreement with me on one point: since abandoning the bisque step, we have witnessed fewer flaws and losses in firing kilns. One theory is that stress at the time of raw glaze application weeds out poorly thrown and overly trimmed vessels. Another hypothesis is that the fewer times clay goes through the ordeal of fire, the less weary and threatened it will be. Bernard Palissy, French painter and potter, stated (in *The Admirable Discourses of B. Palissy,* 1580), "I baked my vessels for the first firing: but when it came to the second firing, I had sorrows and labors such as no man would believe."[6]

GLAZE LIST

The following raw glaze recipes have been selected out of my correspondence with potters over the last four years. The ingredients are calculated by weight unless indicated otherwise. Temperatures are calibrated in Orton cones. Each recipe is noted with a recommended time of application—leather-hard or

40. Tuscarora Pottery School kiln yard.

dry. Glazes noted for leather-hard can normally be applied to wet or soft leather pieces if the glaze consistency is thicker. (British equivalents of the following materials are noted in parentheses.)

As with any new glaze, always try samples before committing the kilnload. Wide variation in fired color and success can be attributed to differences in glaze materials, clay body composition, and kiln fuel.

PAUL SOLDNER

Low-fire White Slip

cone 010 oxidation or reduction
(Parts by volume)

Gerstley borate (colemanite)	1
silica	1
china clay	4

Apply to leather-hard or dry clay.

Low-fire Glaze

cone 010 oxidation or reduction
(Parts by volume)

Gerstley borate (colemanite)	1
china clay	1
borax	1

Apply to dry clay. "Called 'Hendry,' after Ken, of course."

BETTY WOODMAN

Clear Lead Glaze

cone 08 oxidation

lead carbonate	66
silica	30
kaolin	4
bentonite	2

"plus Elmer's glue to hold glaze on pot."
Apply to dry clay.

SUZI CURTIS

Clear Galena Glaze

cone 04–03 oxidation

galena	45.0
lead bisilicate	45.0
ball clay (SMD)	17.5
Cornish stone	2.0
bentonite	3.0

Apply to leather-hard clay. "The addition of 2.5 iron oxide gives an excellent honey glaze. For use on the outside of pots only. Gives good varied quality to the slip."

Clear Frit Glaze

cone 04–03 oxidation

lead bisilicate	70
local clay, earthenware rich in iron and lime	10
Cornish stone	4
whiting	2
bentonite	1
ball clay (SMD)	5

Apply to leather-hard clay. "For use on the inside surfaces of pots—lead release nil or negligible."

Honey Frit Glaze

cone 04–01 oxidation

lead bisilicate	68
local clay	26
Cornish stone	2
whiting	2

Apply to leather-hard clay. "For use on the inside surfaces of pots—lead release nil or negligible."

TONY EVANS

Clear Glaze for Use over Slips

cone 1 oxidation

lead sesquisilicate	80
ball clay	18
whiting	5
flint	5
Cornish stone	5
red iron oxide	6

Apply to leather-hard or dry clay. "Ambre colour."

ALAN FREWIN (Courtesy of *Ceramic Review*)

Slipware Glaze

cone 1 oxidation

lead monosilicate, or lead frit with low melting point	48
clay, preferably the same clay as the body	47
whiting	5

Apply to leather-hard clay. "As a rough guide, the maturing temperature depends on the type of clay and lead frit used. The whiting is not essential but helps to increase the firing range. . . . Red clay will make the glaze show yellow over a white slip."

LYNN MADDOX

Transparent Green Liner Glaze
cone 4–10 oxidation or reduction or salt
colemanite	50
Cornwall stone	50

plus "a little kaolin or Albany or ochre, etc."
 Apply to dry clay.

Transparent Green-Brown Liner Glaze
cone 4–10 oxidation or reduction or salt
colemanite	50
Albany or Barnard clay	25
ball clay	25

 Apply to dry clay.

Clear Liner Glaze
cone 5–10 oxidation or reduction or salt
plastic vitrox clay	50
colemanite	50

plus "a good handful of Alberhill clay."
 Apply to dry clay.

STEVE AND ANN KILBORN

Clear Glaze for Slipware
cone 5–6 oxidation
spodumene	40
Gerstley borate (colemanite)	20
flint	25
Tennessee ball clay	15
dolomite	10

 Apply to leather-hard clay. "For a yellow, which goes gold over a yellow slip, add two percent iron oxide."

JOHN GREEN

White Glossy Glaze
cone 6 oxidation
Gerstley borate (colemanite)	600
Kingman feldspar	400
ball clay	300
zircopax	100
tin	50

 Apply soon after the pot is thrown "with a wide brush, mixed at about the same thickness as sour cream. This gives me a good base for colorants or white background for low-fire commercial decals."

ANDRÉE VALLEY

Gronberg Matt White Glaze
cones 6–9
Kingman feldspar	150
flint	10
kaolin	50
whiting	60
zinc oxide	30

 Apply to dry clay.

JERE LYKINS

White Slip
cone 6–11 oxidation or reduction or salt
Grolleg kaolin	50
Custer feldspar	25
flint	25
bentonite	2

 Apply to wet, leather-hard, or dry clay. "Add color to 'taste.'" Ten percent rutile yields honey color and a half-percent of cobalt yields blue.

SUZI CURTIS

Copper Red Glaze
cone 8 reduction
soda feldspar	30
talc	20
whiting	15
ball clay (SMD)	35
quartz	17
bentonite	5
copper oxide	1
tin	2

 Apply to leather-hard clay.

RICHARD MACKEY

Aki hai Glaze
cone 8 oxidation or reduction
common firebox ash	40
Albany clay	60
iron oxide	5

 Apply to leather-hard or dry clay. Green in reduction; speckled brown or black in oxidation.

RAY GARDINER

Crystalline Yellow Glaze (Credited to Suzi Curtis)
cone 8–9 reduction
ball clay (SMD)	34.3

talc	28.6
whiting	20.0
nepheline syenite	17.1
red iron oxide	3.4

Apply inside to leather-hard and outside to dry clay. "Matt ochre yellow or turns more to give gold specks on dark honey."

ANDRÉE VALLEY

4-D Glaze

cones 8–10

Custer feldspar	65
whiting	10
kaolin	10
bentonite	2
flint	8
dolomite	5
rutile	6
iron	6

Apply to dry clay.

KATHARINE PLEYDELL-BOUVERIE
(Courtesy of *Ceramic Review*)

Raw Ash Glaze

cone 8–10 reduction

ash	5
potash feldspar	5
ball clay	4
quartz	4

"For stoneware brushed on bone-dry raw body pots. Usually fits a raw pot best because the ball clay alone shrinks the glaze better than the mixtures of china clay and ball clay."

JOHN DAVIES (Courtesy of *Ceramic Review*)

Wood Ash Glaze

cone 9–10 reduction

soda feldspar	35
mixed ash	35
ball clay	15
talc	10
quartz	10
bentonite	4

Apply to leather-hard clay. "Used over low-iron bodies, gives a nice warm ochre-green colour. Used over high-iron bodies, gives a splendid golden-green colour and will turn blue where thickest."

RAY GARDINER

Opaque White Glaze

cone 9 reduction

ball clay (SMD)	30
potash feldspar	60
dolomite	22
china clay	15
quartz	9

Apply inside to leather-hard and outside to dry clay. "A very reliable opaque white with a silky surface, good over dark iron slip (I use Leach Slip: 75 red clay/25 red iron oxide)."

RICHARD MACKEY

Mary's Waxy Glaze

cone 9 oxidation or reduction

Custer feldspar	80
whiting	20
copper carbonate	4
ball clay	15

Apply to dry clay. Oxidation: green. Reduction: red. Glossy.

Nukamusuri Glaze

cone 9 oxidation or reduction

rice or rye straw ash	40
Custer feldspar	30
pine ash, washed	30

Apply to dry clay. "Speckled cream color in oxidation or reduction. . . . rather flaky glaze but very beautiful."

Celadon Glaze

cone 9 reduction

F-4 feldspar	44
whiting	18
kaolin	10
flint	28
Albany clay	12

Apply to dry clay. "Light green celadon glaze—smooth."

ANDRÉE VALLEY

Apple Ash Glaze

cone 9

apple ash	35
feldspar	40
ball clay	25

bentonite 2
red iron oxide 2

Apply to dry clay.

PHYLLIS IHRMAN

Adjusted Albany Slips

cone 9-10 oxidation or reduction

Albany clay	90.0	90	90	80	70
feldspar	2.5	—	—	—	—
ball clay	2.5	5	—	10	20
umber	—	5	10	10	10
red iron oxide	5.0	—	—	—	—

Apply to leather-hard clay. "For use over and under glazes. Makes very good glazes when used thick."

#1 Celadon Glaze

cone 9-10 reduction

potash feldspar	40
dolomite	15
bentonite B	20
flint	20
bone ash	5

Apply to leather-hard clay, medium thickness. ". . . for porcelain or stoneware—a blue-white translucent celadon. Use one-fourth to one and a half red iron oxide for darker colors."

#2 Celadon Glaze

cone 9-10 reduction

potash feldspar	60
dolomite	15
bentonite B	20
nepheline syenite	5

Apply to leather-hard clay, medium-to-thick application. ". . . for porcelain or stoneware; cone 9, a soft, translucent celadon with a heavy crackle; cone 10, shiny translucent. Works well over carving. Use one-fourth to two percent iron oxide for a blue-gray to a dark green. Use one-fourth percent red copper oxide and one percent tin oxide for a copper red."

#6 Glaze (Credited to John A. Foster)

cone 9-10 oxidation or reduction

potash feldspar	35
whiting	20
ball clay, Ky OM #4	30
flint	15

Apply to leather-hard clay, medium thickness. ". . . for porcelain or stoneware. A soft satin, translucent, with a tiny crackle."

#7 Glaze (Credited to John A. Foster)

cone 9-10 oxidation or reduction

potash feldspar	35
whiting	20
ball clay, Ky OM #4	35
flint	10

Apply to leather-hard clay, medium thickness. ". . . for porcelain and stoneware. A satin matt, large crackle."

#8 Glaze

cone 9-10 oxidation or reduction

potash feldspar	40
whiting	10
bentonite B	25
flint	10
dolomite	15

Apply to leather-hard clay. Satin opaque at cone 9; satin translucent at cone 10.

Opaque White Glaze

cone 9-10 oxidation or reduction

feldspar	30
whiting	15
dolomite	10
ball clay	30
kaolin	5
flint	10

Apply to leather-hard clay.

MIKE DODD (Courtesy of *Ceramic Review*)

For Raw Glazing

cone 8-10 reduction

local earthenware or iron clay (low-firing)
feldspar potash
wood ash, mixed

} equal parts

Apply to leather-hard clay. "Different combinations will give matt or runny results. Local granite dust, river iron, chalk, ochres, flint, feldspar, and wood ash, ball clay, local earthenware clay, and china clay is all we use for glazes. Some common sense, luck, and experiment is for me the best and most reliable recipe and great fun."

LAURIE AND ANNE McMICHAEL
(Courtesy of *Ceramic Review*)

Satin Matt

cone 9-10 reduction

feldspar, potash 25

nepheline syenite 15
china clay 20
flint 15
dolomite 20
whiting 5
bentonite 3

Apply to leather-hard clay.

ANDRÉE VALLEY

White Liner Glaze
cone 9–10
Custer feldspar 34.7
dolomite 19.6
whiting 3.1
china clay 23.6
flint 18.9

Apply to dry clay. "I don't use many glazes, but my favorite is a white liner. Buttery texture at cone 9."

Kwayes Celadon Glaze
cone 9–10
Custer feldspar 70
whiting 14
flint 14
bentonite 3
iron oxide 0–2%

Apply to dry clay.

Fake Irabo Glaze
cone 9–10
Albany clay 50
whiting 20
barium carbonate 20
flint 10
rutile 4
red iron oxide 2

Apply to dry clay.

Yellow Ash Glaze
cone 9–10
ash 50
Albany clay 50

Apply to dry clay.

St. John's Gold-Fleck Glaze (Credited to Rick St.John)
cone 9–11
Buckingham feldspar 30
flint 20
whiting 10
yellow ochre 10

Apply to dry clay.

ANDREW HOLDEN

Glaze 1
cone 9–11 reduction
potash feldspar 50
ball clay 30
whiting 10
talc 10

Apply to leather-hard clay. Buttery texture.

Glaze 2
cone 9–11 reduction
ball clay 36
whiting 28
potash feldspar 8
quartz/flint 25
talc 3

Apply to leather-hard clay. "A very high lime glaze, which can produce some unusual colours with the addition of varying amounts of iron."

Glaze 3
cone 9–11 reduction
potash feldspar 45
whiting 25
ball clay 20
quartz 10
talc 2
bone ash 3
bentonite 3

Apply to leather-hard clay.

DAVID CORNELL

SPOD Glaze
cone 9–11 reduction
Kingman feldspar 30
spodumene 20
dolomite 25
E. P. Kaolin 20
whiting 5

Apply to dry clay. "... orange to tan to brown with white, depending on iron content of body they're put over and degree of reduction they receive in fire—thicker/white; thinner/dark."

Dolomat Glaze
cone 10 reduction
Kingman feldspar	50
E.P. Kaolin	25
dolomite	25

Application and effects same as SPOD glaze above.

Mamo Glaze
cone 9–11 oxidation or reduction
Kingman feldspar	50
E. P. Kaolin	25
dolomite	20
whiting	5

Apply to dry clay. White matt.

Cornell Blue Glaze
cone 9–11 oxidation or reduction
whiting	50
Kingman feldspar	30
E. P. Kaolin	20

plus 1.5% cobalt carbonate

Apply to dry clay. ". . . a dry, somewhat muted cobalt blue matt."

PETER SOHNGEN

Cornell Blue Matt Glaze
cone 10 reduction
whiting	50
Custer feldspar	30
ball clay	20
cobalt oxide	0.75

Apply thin to dry clay. "Broken blue with possibilities of green and yellow."

Bleached Albany Glaze
cone 10 reduction
Albany clay	32
kaolin	8
whiting	10

Apply to dry clay. "Broken green and yellow and brown color; satin matt."

Soft Albany Glaze I
cone 10 reduction
Albany clay	200
wollastonite	80
kaolin	23
rutile	8

Apply thin to dry clay. "Bright transparent, greenish color; very fluid."

Perri's Black Glaze
cone 10 reduction
Albany clay	75
nepheline syenite	15
barium carbonate	10
iron oxide	2

Apply to dry clay.

Cushing Black Glaze
cone 10 reduction
Albany clay	65
nepheline syenite	10
barium carbonate	10
talc	15
iron oxide	1
manganese oxide	1
cobalt oxide	1
chrome oxide	2

Apply to dry clay.

Hara's AL-2 Glaze
cone 10 reduction
Albany clay	60
silica	13
whiting	10
Buckingham feldspar	12
tin oxide	2
iron oxide	5

Apply to dry clay.

Eustes White Liner Glaze
cone 10 reduction
Custer feldspar	34.7
dolomite	19.6
whiting	3.1
E. P. Kaolin	23.6
silica	18.9

Apply to dry clay.

Shaner Red Glaze
cone 10 reduction
Custer feldspar	58.8
talc	4.8
E. P. Kaolin	27.6
bone ash	4.5
whiting	24.0
iron oxide	4.8
bentonite	2.4

Apply to dry clay.

Stony Matt Glaze
cone 10 reduction
Kona F-4 feldspar	67

dolomite 34
talc 21
spodumene 14
barium carbonate 9
ball clay (#1 SGP) 30

Apply to dry clay.

Steve Hill's Celadon Glaze
cone 10 reduction
Kona F-4 feldspar 33
whiting 20
Albany clay 30
barium carbonate 2
silica 35
ball clay 10
bentonite 5
iron oxide 2

Apply to dry clay.

Smoky Glaze
cone 10 reduction
Albany clay 100
Kingman potash feldspar 100
whiting 20
rutile 4

Apply to dry clay.

JIM ALLEN

Jim's Clear Glaze
cone 10 reduction
potash feldspar 29.5
whiting 22.6
E. P. Kaolin 17.8
flint 30.1

Apply to dry clay. "An excellent base glaze. With nine and a half percent red iron oxide it gives a good tenmoku."

Rhodes' Matt Glaze
cone 10 reduction
potash feldspar 48.9
E. P. Kaolin 25.1
dolomite 22.4
whiting 3.5

Apply to dry clay. "This is a well-known bisque glaze. I found it works perfectly for single-fire."

PHYLLIS IHRMAN

#3 Celadon Glaze
cone 10 reduction
potash feldspar 45
dolomite 7
talc 3
bone ash 5
ball clay, Ky OM #4 35
kaolin 5

Apply to leather-hard clay, medium-to-thick application. ". . . porcelain and stoneware, very soft satin-matt celadon."

#4 Tenmoku and Adventurine Glaze
cone 10 reduction

	A	B
Albany clay	90.0	90.0
feldspar	2.5	2.5
ball clay, Ky OM #4	2.5	2.5
black iron oxide	9.0	5.0
titanium oxide	5.0	5.0

Apply to leather-hard clay, medium thickness. ". . . for porcelain and stoneware. #4A: reddish brown with black and green streaks. #4B: reddish brown matrix with darker silver-brown crystals."

SANDRA JOHNSTONE

Pumpkin Glaze
cone 10 reduction
Kingman feldspar 5½
whiting 1½
barium carbonate 1¼
kaolin 1¼
silica ⅜
iron ⅛
rutile ¾
bentonite ¼

Apply to dry clay. "A perfect glaze for flameware —*won't craze* . . . good on regular stoneware, too. Sometimes orange, sometimes rutile/iron blue. The blue is great but depends on various things: (1) amount of iron in the clay (less iron, more blue); (2) kiln atmosphere (lots of heat and reduction)."

Albany Slip Glaze
cone 10 reduction
feldspar 15
Albany clay 63
whiting 11
silica 6
iron 5

Apply to dry clay. "Lots of clay—good for green glazing. Works in any atmosphere, best in reduction—more variation. Will melt below cone 5 if it's not too thick, can fire well above cone 10."

ROSEMARY CAPES

Tenmoku-Type Glaze

cone 10–11 reduction

earthenware clay	50
feldspar	50

Apply to dry clay. "Glaze really united with body, shiny, lustrous, lightish brown/greenish, textured, smooth, no pinholes, no crawling, no runs, no crazing. Away from flame glaze is black, opaque, semi-matt, slight lustrous sheen, red specking; iron oxide painting shows smooth red on the black ground. Elsewhere in kiln in between the two extremes rather heavy looking, do well to relieve with unglazed foot . . . add fifteen ash to it and fires green/yellow/mottled, useful for cooler parts."

Matt and Textured Glaze

cone 10–11 reduction

earthenware clay	50
feldspar	25
whiting	25

Apply to dry clay. "Goes from pale yellow to dark brown, depending on position in kiln."

JERE LYKINS

Brown Liner Glaze

cone 10–11 reduction

Albany clay	80
ball clay, Ky OM #4	10
yellow ochre	10

Apply to leather-hard clay. Reddish brown satin matt to gloss, depending on temperature.

White Liner Glaze

cone 10–11 reduction

Cornwall stone	50
ball clay	30
whiting	10
flint	10

Apply to leather-hard clay. Off-white to cream gloss translucent.

MARCIA AND DON SKOLNICK-SIMONSON

Jose Dovis' Glossy Clear Glaze #1

cone 11 oxidation or reduction

flint	32.23%
Custer feldspar	22.98
kaolin	14.88
zinc oxide	14.07
whiting	13.19
spodumene	2.64

Apply to wet or leather-hard clay. "We add Calgon: one teaspoon per gallon of glaze (approx.). In oxidation: opaque white. In reduction: clear, grayish."

LARRY SHEP

Ivory Goo or One, Two, Three Glaze

cone 10–12 reduction

plastic vitrox clay	1
ball clay, Ky OM #4	2
talc, Warm Springs 200	3

Apply to wet, soft leather or partial leather-hard clay "never after plasticity is gone or after color changes. In order to assure fit to body the variant is the ball clay. Substitute bentonite for some of the ball clay. Ivory color, buttery smooth opaque like Sara Lee sugar frosting. We add cobalt, iron, tin-vanadium-indium stain for colors which are mainly matt."

Other glaze recipes are listed in the index.

CHAPTER 4

Other Approaches: Variations in Single-Firing

SALT GLAZE

It was through working with salt glazing that I was led into glazing raw as a general studio practice. From my correspondence I have learned that I was not alone on the path. A potter who bisques before salting is looked on as an oddity. "Why would he want to do that? What's the advantage?"

The basis for this marriage between single- and salt-firing rests on clear historical precedence and the nature of vapor glazing. Every manual that refers back to the origins of our salt-glazing tradition goes on to remind us that the pieces needed only one firing. Since the atmosphere in a salt kiln glazes the ware, the necessity is gone for applying glaze. Water-base slips or glazes that are used generally go on in flourishes rather than coats. When you put a liquid onto raw clay, the characteristic problems that can arise multiply in direct proportion to the area of clay covered.

For a studio potter, glazing with salt has one serious drawback—that relentless war sodium wages on firebricks. The principle of this type of firing is that when sodium chloride is thrown into a kiln, heat releases the sodium into a vapor. As this wisps over and around the pottery, it fluxes silica in the surface of the clay and forms glaze. With each new kilnload, the old firebricks absorb another attack. The inevitable outcome is that salt kilns do not live as long as other kilns. The practice can be justified economically only if the prices you receive for this ware are inflated to cover the preordained loss of equipment.

The contemporary lure of salt is as much due to its serendipity as for its unique product. There are so many variables in a firing. With experience most of these can be manipulated, others predicted, and a few conceded. The results you get can be controlled through clay-body composition, amount of salt introduced, distribution of vapor (kiln design and stacking pattern), fuel, and rate of cooling. Speculation on other, undiscovered factors continues. Therefore, if a potter tells you that with his clay body a piece *will* come out light gray with rust blushes and a small orange-peel texture—what he means is *sometimes, should,* or *you come to expect.* . . .

Salt Clay

Almost any clay body will form glaze in a salt firing. The common stoneware recipes that fire out "toasty" with iron spots in a reduction kiln will come out of a salt firing covered with a dark brown, chocolate-syrup glaze. Such a background limits decorative possibilities by muting any other colors from applied oxides or glazes. For the same reason that painters buy light-colored canvases, potters show partiality for gray-to-white salt-glazed stoneware. For

41. "Lydia Dwight," by John Dwight, the potter credited with introducing salt glaze to England in 1671. Salt-glazed stoneware. (*Crown Copyright. Victoria and Albert Museum, London*)

variety I keep the following three mixtures on hand:

1. fireclay	100 lbs.
ball clay	50 lbs.
feldspar	25 lbs.
silica	10 lbs.
magnesium carbonate	5 lbs.
plus sand and mica	

Results: Warm, toasty, orange to brown.

2. fire clay	50 lbs.
ball clay	50 lbs.
XX saggar clay	50 lbs.
feldspar	20 lbs.
silica	20 lbs.
magnesium carbonate	5 lbs.
plus sand and mica	

Results: Lighter, warm gray with pale orange blush.

3. fire clay	50 lbs.
ball clay	50 lbs.
feldspar	50 lbs.
silica	50 lbs.
plus sand and mica	

Results: White to gray-green.

The amount of sand and mica you add is determined by what is to be made from the clay. Both ingredients, in moderation, will increase the wet strength while slightly decreasing the plasticity. If I plan to throw large vessels or handbuild, I add 20 to 25 pounds of 60-mesh sand and an equal volume of mica. But when I have orders for mugs and dinner plates, ten pounds or less make a more sensitive clay.

All three bodies are easy to salt, *i.e.*, the glaze

42. Salt-glazed stoneware covered jar, by Lynn Maddox. Height 12 inches (30.5 cm.). (*Tom Maddox*)

builds up early and remains bright even in a heavily salted firing. This is because the mixtures are high in silica and during firing are rendered vitreous by the presence of flux (magnesium carbonate and/or feldspar).

Decoration

Slips by definition have a high clay content and by virtue of this are a good medium for decorating any raw ware—clay on clay. Those slips relatively high in alumina are admired for their stability in a salt firing. Without sufficient alumina to resist the fluxing vapors, any band of color, design, or crisp brushwork will bleed and flow.

To prevent color migration, German potters have an old rule of thumb: add one-third or more clay to an oxide. Before I learned of this, I was into the habit of diluting oxides in a basic porcelain slip:

kaolin	25
ball clay	25
feldspar	25
silica	25

and added for color:

cobalt	1	bright blue
copper	5	red or green (unreliable)
chrome	4	bright green
iron	8	brown
rutile	10	yellow with traces of all above

Glazes used in salt must also contain enough alumina so that the extra fluxing will not melt them off the pot and onto the kiln shelf. Expect the characteristics of your glaze—color, opacity, and brilliance—to change. Avoid recipes calling for a high percentage of whiting as these are apt to blister. For all these reasons, test glazes on a few pieces before risking all your work and your kiln shelves.

A reliable glaze for salt evolved from the porcelain slip. Since porcelain as a clay body is calculated to be vitreous and translucent, the recipe seemed a logical starting point for developing a white salt glaze:

43. "Kimberlite Pipe," by Andrée Valley. Vapor-glazed colored porcelains. 1976. Height 13 inches (33 cm.). (*Bob Kalmbach*)

kaolin	10
ball clay	10
feldspar	50
silica	25
plus Gersley borate (colemanite)	10
talc	10
zinc	3

As slip, the porcelain recipe could be applied either thick or thin onto leather-hard clay; because of its high clay content it could only be applied rather thin on bone-dry ware. Reducing the amounts of kaolin and ball clay adjusts it into a thick slip for dry pots. The addition of supplementary fluxes takes the slip one step further into a glaze that melts without salt, but a glaze that is stiff enough not to run if fluxed by sodium fumes. The zinc, though a flux, was included mainly because it enhances and clarifies cobalt blues. The final recipe has been frequently tampered with in other ways, for different reasons, and I hear that it always works —basically too simple to fail.

Salt glazing is as much a separate aesthetic as it is a technique; it is not the way for every potter, every vessel. Thought should go into the char-

44. Salt-glazed stoneware cup and saucer, by Jere Lykins. White liner glaze on interior. (*Jere Lykins*)

acteristics of salt glaze. "What is unique about the surface? Can I take advantage of its virtues? What shapes work best? Why salt this piece?" My tenet is that if the same decorative results you desire can come out of a vaporless kiln, do not waste the precious space in a short-lived salt kiln.

The Kiln

For converting a kiln to salt or building a new one, be certain you are in possession of good-quality firebricks rated for several hundred degrees above the projected end temperature. Soft insulation bricks will melt. Exotic bricks containing 60 to 90 percent alumina have not been proven to me to be worth their high prices. A personal example: Kruzite D firebricks (A. P. Green) have a 70 percent alumina content and are rated for cone 37. After six salt firings these bricks were still unglazed and showed no ill effect. However, thirty-six saltings later they had swollen and bloated, and their surfaces were covered with dry scales. Admittedly there was no shiny evidence of glaze formation. But these scales, like petrified elm leaves, would fall from the arch during firing, adhering tenaciously to the pots they landed in and on.

Because the initial cost of these high alumina bricks was three times what I normally paid, I resolved never again. Of course, I hear the claims made by employees of brick companies, and by some potters, that the firebricks, castable refractory, or fiber insulation they have will resist salt. I do not say they lie, but such testimonials remind me of a couple saying how they are so happily married after only two or three years trying. I want to hear the story of a potter and his old salt kiln. For the price of exotic insulation I can melt and rebuild three kilns of ordinary firebricks.

To delay the inevitable, I paint the inside face of the bricks with a thick wash of alumina and kaolin, 1:1. The kiln is then fired several times as a reduction kiln to seal the brick surface. This helps to prevent deep penetration of salt vapor. When the firebox and walls show evidence of wear, they are touched-up with wash; the arch is never recoated. Stalactites form and release occasional droplets of a thick Albany-like glaze. Thankfully, this unpredictable, Zen decoration is smooth and glassy—so long as it originates on an arch that has not been layered with repeated coats of high alumina wash.

To save your kiln shelves and posts, pots can be loaded in the kiln without furniture (lip to lip, foot to foot, and lip to foot) with the contact points separated by pads of kiln-wash putty. This practice is difficult to institute in an American school-studio where variety rather than uniformity is the ideal. Here, with a multitude of sizes and shapes, handbuilt and thrown, to be arranged in the same kiln, shelves are indispensable.

Brush a double coat of kiln wash on the topside of silicon carbide shelves and then, though deterioration is noticed in glassy build-up and in eventual warpage, most shelves will outlive your kiln. The glass that forms on the underside and edges of silicon carbide should be ground off with a handstone after each firing to prevent dripping in the next.

By dipping posts and door bricks in the wash, you can add many firings to their lives. If used firebricks are employed as posts, be certain they were not part of an earlier salt kiln.

Even bricks without the obvious signs of having been salted (such as bricks used for the outside layer on a double-walled salt kiln) may have been permeated by sodium fumes. These will melt from the inside out when fired up to 2300° F. (1260° C.).

Firing

First firings are always filled with mystery. After several firings a salt kiln will have told you where glaze buildup is heavy, medium, and light. Thereafter, pots can be placed in the kiln on the basis of how much glaze you want each to collect. Wide spaces can be left open horizontally between the pots, and also vertically between the lip of the tallest piece and the shelf above for free circulation of vapors. This way fewer pots are fired, but such a loose stacking promotes an even development of glaze throughout the kiln. Or the opposite may be done. Load pieces as close to one another as possible and thus encourage irregular patterns of glaze.

Any form of salt can be used: table salt, rock salt, or water-softener pellets. An addition of between three and ten percent borax hastens glaze buildup, as does a little water—just enough to moisten the crystals.

I mix this in a bucket as the kiln is approaching cone 8. Between cone 8 and cone 10, I shovel small amounts through the salt ports. By throwing it in before the final cone has bent, I can ascertain that the temperature is still climbing, albeit slowly. Should the temperature of the ware drop sharply, the vapor will recrystallize rather than flux, depositing a residue of salt scum in the bottoms of pots.

Slow, regular salting prevents that happening. My conservative schedule calls for throwing in roughly two pounds of rock salt; pushing the dampers closed for five minutes to trap the fumes; pulling the dampers open, and leaving them that way for the next five minutes. This raises the temperature and clears the kiln. I continue the three-step regime until the thickness of glaze I desire appears.

The judgment is made by pulling draw rings. For this purpose I arrange three clay rings, made from the same clay body as the majority of the ware, in front of each cone pad. After half of the predicted amount of salt has been used, I hook one of the rings with a long metal rod and pull it out to check on the growth of the glaze. Final determination on the amount of salt needed is my satisfaction with these samples, rather than any preconceived notion of how much salt *should* be used, or how many hours salting *should* take.

Caution: Throwing damp salt into a hot kiln creates steam—*suddenly*, and sometimes it provokes violent back pressure out the salt port. Goggles are sensible protective gear to wear.

The color of salt glaze on raw clay is to a large degree predetermined by the amount of iron present in the constituents that made up the clay body. But colors can be influenced by

45. A salt-glaze kiln loaded without furniture. Studio of Sandra Johnstone. (*Sandra Johnstone*)

whether a kiln is fired in oxidation or reduction, and by how rapidly the kiln is cooled. Lighter colors are fostered by an oxidation firing followed by a quick cooling down to dull red heat. The latter is accomplished by leaving dampers and burner ports open until the temperature drops to about 1100° F. (600° C.), then closing all the openings until the kiln is cool enough to have the door unbricked.

Among urban potters, sodium bicarbonate (soda) has become a popular substitute for sodium chloride (salt). The advantage of the switch is that soda does not produce the hallmark billowy white clouds from chimneys. The drawback is that the quality of glass made with soda is not the same; the classic orange-peel texture is often missing; some pots come out looking as if they had only a thin spray of clear gloss glaze.

The distribution of soda vapors is also spotty. One side of a piece may be glassy while the other side is semi-matt. These problems are caused by the slow and often incomplete vaporization of soda. Mixtures of soda and salt can adjust a compromise between glaze texture and fumes. Sal soda and soda ash can also be sources of sodium vapor, but they act similarly to sodium bicarbonate. These substitutes work best when introduced into the kiln for their uniqueness rather than as an ersatz salt. It is true that nothing makes salt glaze like salt.

The only fuel that imposes itself on salt glaze is wood. I cannot identify differences between pieces fired with gas, diesel or crankcase oil; with wood there are discernible deposits of ash that mix in with glaze. This contamination accentuates the glaze texture on shoulders, tints it green and, in extreme cases, causes heavy streaking. The effect of wood can be seen on pots in the top of a kiln even when the fuel was used only in the early stages of firing.

Toward the end of a salt firing there are at least two decorative tricks that can be practiced. The first creates a red glaze, sometimes. Any source of copper dropped in the hot firebox will give off fumes. As these circulate through the kiln they settle here or there on the molten glazes, infusing a few with a blush of plum red. When the burners are turned off, the kiln should be allowed to cool slowly.

My original experiments with copper fuming were at a time when friends were bronze casting and they would bring me the solidified slag ladled off before the pour. Today I keep my eyes open for odd brass plumbing parts, spigots and valves, short sections of copper tubing and coils of abandoned telephone line. Of course, copper carbonate or oxide will do the job, but these are expensive and their toxic fumes far more concentrated than those coming from an old faucet.

The second poisonous fuming agent, and the most popular, is stannous chloride. The

46. Salt-glazed stoneware churn, by J. D. Craven; North Carolina, late nineteenth century. Fired with wood. Height 15 inches (38.1 cm.). Author's collection. (*Valerie Parks*)

47. Egyptian paste-inscribed ushabti; Abydos, Egypt, Dynasty XXX. (*Courtesy The Oriental Institute, University of Chicago*)

intention is to luster glaze with a transparent film of mother-of-pearl. Two or more teaspoonsful are tossed into the firebox just as the kiln is cooling from red to black—too soon and the fumes dissipate with no effect, too late and the surface of the glaze scums over. Again the results are spotty because of the nature of the carrier—vapor drafting through shelves filled with ware, touching a pot here and missing the one next to it.

The smoke from a salt kiln, with no hazardous additives, has a poor reputation. Though I have yet to talk with a salt glaze potter who has experienced or witnessed an illness related to firing, persistent rumors circulate about how these kilns expel deadly chlorine gas. To ease my conscience when I was a college teacher, I went directly to the chairman of the Chemistry Department for consultation. He gave the most reassuring summary by explaining that, yes, sodium chloride when heated will produce chlorine gas, but that happens only in the absence of H_2O. With any water present, even humidity in the air, the end product will be a gaseous form of hydrochloric acid which "in such dilute form is probably not harmful and might even have a beneficial cleansing action on the lungs."

Though comforted, I continue to recommend standing upwind when firing a salt kiln (for that matter, any kiln). If proven or questionable toxic agents are present in the firing, wear a mask.

SELF-GLAZING CLAY

Self-glazing clay is a ceramic material which is a composite of both clay and glaze. In its moist state it is plastic enough to be formed into objects, usually beads. Later, as the body dries, the glaze ingredients work their way to the surface to form a fluxing skin. I make mention of this specialty first because it is single-fired, and secondly because pieces made from it have distinctive characteristics—more akin to jewelry than pottery.

Today the medium is most commonly enjoyed as amusement, rarely as the sole means of making a living. In fact, one potter who has employed self-glazing clays on and off for several years wrote me saying, "Self-glazing clay is a real pain . . . for anyone working with their hands."

The practice originated in Egypt sometime around 5000 B.C. as the first recorded use of glaze on clay, and the tradition has continued uninterrupted to this day. The basis of Egyptian paste is a mixture high in silica with sufficient sodium for fluxing and some plasticity for modeling. As the compound dries its soluble salts migrate to the outer surfaces where they collect as a fuzzy coating (fragile like the texture of mold on cheese) that melts in firing.

Many recipes exist. These two are adapted from *The Ceramic Review Book of Glaze Recipes*:

SYLVIA HYMAN Cone 012

nepheline syenite	39
silica	37
soda ash	6
sodium bicarbonate	6
kaolin	6
ball clay	6
bentonite	2
add—	
copper carbonate	2%—turquoise
cobalt	¼%–1%—blue
chromium oxide	½%–1%—green
uranium oxide	2%–6%—yellow
	10%–20%—orange
manganese dioxide	½%–2%—gray violet

ALICIA FELBERBAUM Cone 07

feldspar	34
silica	34
soda ash	5
sodium bicarbonate	5
kaolin	5
bentonite	4
add—	
copper oxide	3%—turquoise (greener)
copper carbonate	3%—turquoise (darker)
manganese	3%—mauve purple
chrome	3%—apple green
iron oxide	3%—salmon pink

A common denominator in all paste recipes is a poor workability which limits the size and complexity of the objects you can make. Water must be added carefully to the dry mix (approximately two tablespoons to 100 grams). If too much is included, the mixture will be limp; too little and it will be crumbly.

A final problem may arise because, though there is a charm to Egyptian paste beads after they are fired, this is dulled if you must load someone else's into your kiln (one by one by one by one). Only the person who formed them can sustain the patience.

Ken Hendry has run experiments to devise a self-glazing clay body capable of being wheel-thrown as well as handbuilt in larger forms, with slabs and coils. Through his research in the studio, he developed several recipes. According to Ken, all the mixes handle about as well as a good porcelain clay. The principles of each are similar. Together with the required sodium fluxes you include: (1) 50 percent fine-grained, plastic clay; (2) up to 20 percent grog; (3) at least 30 percent ground silica.

Fire to cone 6:

#1 Sutter Clay	
Sutter Clay	54
silica	30
colemanite	10
soda ash	2
sodium bicarbonate	2
bentonite	2
#2 "Debra Jordy's Paste"	
Sutter clay	62
silica	30
soda ash	4
sodium bicarbonate	4
#3 Cedar Heights	
Gold Art clay	28
ball clay	28
silica	36
soda ash	3
sodium bicarbonate	3
bentonite	2
#4 Saggar Clay	
ball clay	29
silica	34

PLATE 1
Salt-glazed stoneware urnbag with lid by the author. Height 16 inches (40.6 cm.). 1966. The lid was dipped into white porcelain glaze when clay was dry, and a band of cobalt was brushed on top. (*Valerie Parks*)

PLATE 2
Chinese covered jar; T'ang Dynasty. Height 8 inches (20.3 cm.). Single-fired. Art and History Museum, Shanghai, The People's Republic of China.

PLATE 3
Crock from North Carolina; mid-nineteenth century. Marked "10" gallons. Single-fired. Height 20½ inches (52 cm.). Author's collection. (*Ron Moroni*)

PLATE 4
Jug from North Carolina; mid-nineteenth century. Marked "3" gallons. Single-fired. Height 14½ inches (36.8 cm.). Author's collection. (*Ron Moroni*)

PLATE 5
Churn from North Carolina; mid-nineteenth century. Marked "6" gallons. Single-fired. Height 20 inches (50.8 cm.). Author's collection. (*Ron Moroni*)

PLATE 6
Low-fire voco, by Paul Soldner. "Vessel oriented clay object." Height 20 inches (50.8 cm.). The flashing is a result of this piece being fired in a tightly packed oil kiln where a small amount of salt was introduced at cone 010.

PLATE 7
"Remembrance of Florida," by the author. Stoneware, 7 x 9 inches (17.8 x 22.9 cm.). 1978. The *terra nigra* effect on this wall plaque is the result of its being fired face-down with a square of plywood sandwiched between it and the kiln shelf. (*Ron Moroni*)

PLATE 8
Stoneware wall plaque, by the author. 12½ x 18 inches (31.8 x 45.8 cm.). 1976. The shine on the unglazed clay surface is produced by the contaminants in a drainoil firing. (*Ron Moroni*)

soda ash	3
sodium bicarbonate	3
bentonite	2
add—	
copper	2%—turquoise to green
vanadium stain	5%—lemon yellow
manganese	5%—"an elusive but good purple"
chrome	3%—yellow-green
cobalt	1%—"earthy blue"
rutile	5%—tan

I confess to regarding self-glazing clays as novelties. They remind me of a Swiss Army knife—a combination that is both a can opener and a toenail clipper. But really both of these jobs can be carried out better, more smoothly and more efficiently with separate tools. Another prejudice. Swiss Army knives continue to sustain broad popularity year after year.

TERRA SIGILLATA

No less an authority than the late Cullen W. Parmelee stated that *terra sigillata* "... cannot be classified as an engobe or glaze." Yet he did include, along with this statement, several paragraphs on *terra sigillata* in his classic reference volume, *Ceramic Glazes*. In this same broad sense I would like to outline the technique here as a raw glazing variant.

Actually *terra sigillata* behaves a little like both a slip and a glaze. It is a liquid clay (slip) applied by the familiar methods (brushing, dipping, or spraying) and then fired to a vitrifying temperature, 1650°–1830° F. (900°–1000° C.), though technically the coating does not form glass.

The typical half-glossy, red-brown surface can be seen often in museums on Greco-Roman pottery, and here and there today on pieces in contemporary ceramic exhibitions. William Alexander not only uses *terra sigillata* on his current work, but he is also a technical historian in the field, having researched the subject during his travels throughout the Mediterranean and having participated in several archeological digs. I am indebted to him for these recipes:

Attic Terra Sigillata
red clay	230 grams
Calgon	5 grams
water	1 liter

Alfred Terra Sigillata
red clay	300.0 grams
Calgon	1.5 grams
water	.7 liter

Anonymous Terra Sigillata
red clay	1,168.0 grams
sodium hydroxide	3.28 grams
water	3.0 quarts

Swiss Terra Sigillata
red clay	680.0 grams
sodium hydroxide	1.95 grams
water	3.0 liters

48. *Terra sigillata* basket, by Betty Woodman. Italian earthenware. 1978. Length 20 inches (50.8 cm.). (*Betty Woodman*)

Procedure: Mix Calgon (or sodium hydroxide) in water and then add the clay. If there is lime present in your tap water, use distilled water. Allow the solution to slake down for at least 15 minutes before stirring thoroughly. Next, pour it into a glass container and leave it for a day or two—until you can see that the particles have settled into three fairly distinct layers.

The top layer containing the finest-sized particles is *terra sigillata*. Siphon this off and boil in an open pan to evaporate excess water. If the liquid is to be applied with a brush, its consistency should be thick and creamy. For dipping or spraying, a much thinner mixture is used. Examination of Roman pottery has shown that their coating was only between .2 and .6 mil in thickness.

Because *terra sigillata* is so often applied thin, you seldom encounter the most common raw glazing problem—matching the shrinkage of a liquid to that of the clay body. For the same reason, coordinating the timing of your application to the moisture of the ware becomes less important.

The typical clays *terra sigillata* is made from are low-fire earthenwares that fire out ochre to brick red in color. The microscopic platelets of the clay must be capable of lying closely parallel in order for them to sinter and cement together in firing; therefore, the clays best suited are those composed primarily of flat mica-like particles, *e.g.*, illite and sericite.

The most frequent problem comes after your piece is coated and fired and emerges with no sheen. Here are several remedies to try next time, not necessarily in this order:

—Ball-mill the mixture for four hours or more to reduce the particle size.
—Burnish the coating with a stone before firing.
—After burnishing, buff lightly with baby oil; then fire.
—Add a small percentage of flux (cheating?).

TERRA NIGRA

Terra nigra is not a glaze. It is Latin for black earth: a term applied broadly to all unglazed smoke-black pottery (Plate 7), most of it hand-built and once-fired.

In America when potters gather to banter about their work, *terra nigra* is never mentioned, though it seems to me that a large body of contemporary work falls neatly into such a category (those pieces coming from pit fire and sawdust saggars, and some raku). The definition is open to any clay object the decoration of which relies on excess carbon being deposited in its pores, whether the surface is partially glazed or not. Incidentally, the density of color and any patterns left by the smoke have a low level of predictability.

Since the beginning of ceramic history, blackened pottery has been produced on every continent. The reasons for making such ware are various (including accidents), but the black is always created by the same principle—deprive your combustible of enough oxygen,

49. Chinese pottery excavated in Tuscarora, Nevada; Late Ch'ing Dynasty. Front: opium pipe, *terra nigra*, diameter 2¾ inches (7 cm.); middle: opium pipe, *terra sigillata*, diameter 2¾ inches (7 cm.); back: jar, dark slip glaze, height 5½ inches (14 cm.). Author's collection. (*Valerie Parks*)

then carbon will form and be deposited in your clay. Examples are plentiful: from Neolithic cooking pots to yesterday's raku sculptures. Speculation on the motives of our ancestors, pre-wheel, pre-glaze, pre-kiln potters, is that they probably did not know any better. They followed a naïve system of firing and, therefore, could not avoid blackening their wares. A scene is conjured up of *Urmenschen* dressed in wild animal skins stacking their raw pots in a pile with sticks and straw (over, under, and around), igniting the bonfire with a glowing coal, and standing around feeding the fire with little concern for an efficient ratio of air intake to exhaust.

Nowadays potters go to great effort, inconvenience, and sometimes pain to short-circuit our modern technology in the pursuit of similar results. Here our scene is inside a suburban garage with an electric kiln going. The potter is wearing an asbestos coat and gloves as he opens the lid to the hot kiln, and with long tongs carefully but gingerly transfers a glowing pot from the smokeless soft brick chamber to an adjacent trashcan filled with sawdust. The lid is secured snugly and the clay blackens.

The results of both systems may look alike, but we must assume a divergence in the expectations of potters from different generations and consider the admiration of and utility expected by their public. No preindustrial potters were intentionally taking chances with their ware, their decoration, their livelihood; whereas today a delight in tempting fate is admired. I intend no judgment, merely an observation. Any quick classifying on the one hand craft, and the other ART, is too easy. Ephemeral. Rather I feel that the *lure* of the unpredictable is simply our luxury; one that only potters living in wealthy, industrialized civilizations can afford.

The risk of cracking or blowing up your work during firing decreased as the technology of containing heat advanced. Certainly, permanent kilns were at first devised and later improved upon because of this. We now return to primitive methods as a response to faint philosophical and nostalgic echoes.

Methods

A low-fire *terra nigra* "kiln" can be as basic as a bonfire, a hole in the ground, or a 55-gallon barrel; all are stacked and fired similarly. The pots and the fuel are loaded together in the same manner you carefully pack a shipping crate. For fuel, whatever is handy will do: sawdust, wood chips, sticks, and straw.

By igniting the top of the pile the fire is guaranteed to be inefficient as it slowly burns down. If a barrel contains the fire, a series of holes should be poked around the circumference at the bottom in order to admit enough oxygen for burning. Extra fuel may be required to keep the fire burning for two to three hours. The exact time any firing will take is determined by how hard you want the clay to become.

Usually to produce a dense to vitreous body, a regular kiln with its regular fuel is fired, the pots packed in combustibles and enclosed in saggars. These containers can be either vessel-saggars or brick-saggars. The first type is constructed by handbuilding a slab box and a lid, or by throwing a straight-walled covered jar large enough to hold the objects you wish to smoke. The clay the saggar is made from can be your usual recipe, though repeated firings may cause some saggars to crack. For more permanent saggars, mix a clay body with a high percentage of large particle fireclay and/or saggar clay, rich in grog, with no fluxes.

A brick saggar is built inside your kiln either directly on the floor or on top of kiln shelves. This box acts as support posts for the shelves above, while they in turn serve as the lid.

Both setups are loaded with pots and fuel in the same manner as an outdoor pit firing. If completely blackened pottery is not what you admire, cut small breather holes in the leather-hard vessel-saggar or lay the brick-saggar loosely with spaces. These openings will permit more oxygen to enter the enclosure and when this air unites with carbon, clean gray patterns of the draft are burned into the black.

"Beauty must have some room, must be associated with freedom. Freedom, indeed *is* beauty. The love of the irregular is a sign of the basic quest for freedom "—Sōetsu Yanagi.[7]

CHAPTER 5

Burning Drainoil

WHY NOT FIRE WITH DRAINOIL?

There is a connection between my reverting from bisque to single-firing, and then converting from gas to drainoil for fuel. Fred Elliott ascribed it to a dual tendency to be lazy and cheap. But there is hearsay from other sources to be considered. I have never heard of a potter who fires a bisque kiln with drainoil. All drainoil kilns seem to be owned by raw glazers. Look at those who fire with electricity; bisquing is their rule. Potters firing with gas or diesel exclusively show no discernible fuel-related trend, but wood firers do. The majority of them are raw glazing.

What is this connection between wood and drainoil? There is the subtle relationship between the fired ware; both are likely to be marked with random flashes and blushes by the long, rich flames in the kiln (Plate 8). Physically, the gathering of the two fuels is hard work. No one would want to engage in it more often than need be. Here is a thread that connects back to single-firing.

Firing with drainoil also has one of the same obvious advantages of wood; the fuel is "free." This can extend the economy of single-firing. Whatever costs involved are more likely computed in hours than in dollars and cents. Firing drainoil is not as simple as flipping an electric switch and signing a check at the end of the month. Nor is the process as easy as turning a gas valve and lighting a match.

Gas is the familiar fuel to potters. For good reasons it has been the preferred heat source for kilns in America: clean burning, efficient, easy to control, handy, and (until recently) inexpensive. Whether your gas is butane, methane, natural, or propane—the burners, firing schedule, atmosphere, and results are quite similar. Liquid fuels differ with unique demands and eccentricities. It is essential to understand the basic nature of this "new" fuel, the nomenclature, its safety, and environmental boundaries—as well as simply how to fire with it. I hope my prejudices are straightforward. I have drifted, borrowed, experimented, and, for the present, settled on an oil-firing system that works well for me, today in rural Nevada. A modified pipe burner firing drainoil is simple, inexpensive, and labor intensive. This may not be just the right setup for everyone, so I have included information on optional burners and preheating fuels.

THE NATURE OF OIL

All heating oils are composed of approximately 14 percent hydrogen and 86 percent carbon. These elements must be mixed with oxygen in order for combustion to occur. Oil will not burn when the hydrogen and carbon remain in a dense liquid state. Only after oil has become a gas, combined with air, will it support combustion. This transformation is accomplished by a burner which either vaporizes or atomizes the liquid. The term "carburetor"

50. Drainoil. (*Ron Moroni*)

would be more precise in describing the function of a burner on an oil kiln. In contrast to the common gas venturi burner (where gas and air mix inside the burner and ignite at the tip), the typical oil burner blows a fuel/air mixture into the firebox before combustion takes place. These burners will not sustain a flame outside of the kiln.

The two kinds of oil easily available and currently used in kilns are diesel #2 and drainoil (waste oil, crankcase oil, sump oil). Kerosene is popular abroad but difficult to obtain and prohibitively expensive here. Stove oil is seldom used; though it is slightly more volatile than diesel, it is also more costly. Technically all oils are described and graded by a number of specifications: British thermal unit (Btu), Conradson, distillation, Baumé, sediment/water, pour point, viscosity, and flash point. Of these, viscosity, flash point and Btu are the most important for a potter to learn about prior to deciding on which fuel/burner system to use.

Viscosity refers to the resistance of a fluid to flow and, in the heating industry, is rated by the number of seconds a given amount of oil flows through a standard orifice at 100° F. If the temperature is lowered, the viscosity is raised. Diesel's viscosity is low enough that even when the temperature of your fuel tank is below 0° F., this oil has no problems flowing through pipes to a burner. On the contrary, drainoil, which is already thick and viscous at 100° F., becomes gelatinous at 0° F. In order for it to flow through pipes in the winter it has to either be thinned with a lighter oil or preheated to lower the viscosity.

The flash point of a liquid fuel is the temperature at which, if a match were passed over an open container, the vapors rising off the fuel would momentarily support combustion.

```
kerosene  104° F. (40° C.) flash point
diesel #2 170° F. (76° C.) flash point
drainoil  475° F. (245° C.) flash point
                              (estimated)
```

These figures point to the cause of the ignition and early firing difficulties in burning drainoil. A more flammable fuel with a lower flash point, such as diesel, propane, or wood, must be burned first to raise the temperature in the firebox. Since flash point is the minimum temperature needed to produce a flammable vapor, a higher temperature is necessary to sustain a flame—in excess of 900° F. (470° C.)—before drainoil is blown into a firebox. Flash point is also an indicator of the relative safety with which a fuel can be stored.

The British thermal unit (Btu) is the standard for measuring amounts of heat. One Btu is the quantity of heat needed to raise the temperature of one pound of water by one degree Fahrenheit. Knowledge of a fuel's heat potential allows you to examine and compare fuel options on the basis of how much heat a dollar buys.

Economy

Here is a cost analysis of three fuels (1978 prices). Though the per gallon price of each will always be rising, their relative cost should remain fairly constant.

	Btu	$/gallon	Btu/$
propane	93,500	$.46	203,260
diesel	135,000–139,000	.47	284,234
drainoil	160,000 (estimate)	free	—

The Btu figure for drainoil is a conservative guess. The heaviest heating oil rated is #6 with 155,900 Btu's. But to be fair to the users of propane and diesel, and realistic to potters thinking of switching to drainoil, some cost for time, labor, and hauling should be assessed to drainoil.

Examining my predicament here in Tuscarora gives a rough idea of the hidden costs. I drive a half-ton pickup truck, loaded with three empty 55-gallon barrels, 52 miles to the nearest service stations and return with 165 gallons of drainoil. The round trip takes at least three hours out of the day. Figure:

104 miles @ $.15 per mile	$15.60
3 hours' labor @ $4 per hour	12.00
Total	$27.60 for 165 gallons of fuel
or	$.17/gallon (941,176 Btu/$)

Most potters would not need to drive as far nor take as much time, but then they might wish to ascribe more value to their labor. Details. The inescapable conclusion is that drainoil, dirty and discarded, is a very cheap source of Btu's.

Drawbacks

Now if costs were the sole consideration in choosing a fuel, drainoil would be firing every kiln. Responsible for the fuel's lack of popularity is its smoke, smell, and attendant mess. All oils can be messy: drainoil is naturally the dirtiest. Few mid-century Americans approve of making a mess. Certainly no state-supported school would sanction the practice for long on campus.

Regardless of how fastidious you are in tending an oil firing, by the time the last cone bends you have oil on your hands, under your fingernails, and in your clothes. Since all fuel oils have a distinctive odor, so do you. Burning diesel smells like rush hour on the freeway; drainoil like a long wait in a Greyhound station. Perhaps someday a clever potter will concoct an oil additive (say, essence of pine sap) to give kiln firing the aroma of a campfire. Then mess and odor will no longer be contentious issues.

Oil kilns do smoke more than gas kilns. A fact. But attentively fired they should emit less unburned carbon than a rustic, backcountry, wood kiln. The density of smoke exhausted through a chimney depends upon the efficacy of the fuel/air mixture in the firebox. This in turn is contingent on compatible burner and firebox design, and ultimately on a responsibly tended fire. Under the best conditions, drainoil burns as clean as diesel.

Ecology

Today where there's smoke there is a discussion of ecology.

"Will the fumes from a drainoil firing damage my health?"

"Is wood smoke better than oil smoke?"

"What pollutants are released in the air from a gas firing?"

"Aren't electric kilns the least contaminating?"

Like other problems common to potters (such as bad backs, bursitis, hemorrhoids, and varicose veins), science offers us expert conflicting opinions. We cannot wait for a final solution to environmental pollution: neither can we ignore the fallout. My conscience, my neighbors, the county health inspector, and the Environmental Protection Agency all hover around reminding me. The subject demands thought and study.

In a file labeled "Dangers in Pottery," I store miscellaneous newspaper clippings, articles, and old letters pertaining to subjects like the symptoms of lead poisoning, the prognosis of silicosis, etc. Also, any material I come across that is related to a potter's imposition on his environment, I save. Following are excerpts:

"Converting fossil fuel to electricity wastes energy. Eighty percent of all electricity is generated by fossil fuel . . . 72% of this energy is lost during the generation and transmission process."[8]

"A 30-cubic-foot kiln fired to cone 9 and salted consumes: 30 lbs. natural gas, 570 lbs. air, 25 lbs. salt. . . .

"This 30-cubic-foot kiln produces these effluents in the final two hours of firing: 60.0 lbs. water vapor, 84.0 lbs. carbon dioxide, 456.0 lbs. nitrogen, 1.0 lb. sodium compounds, 13.5 lbs. chlorine as hydrochloric acid and other chlorine compounds. . . .

"With the exception of the sodium and chlorine compounds, the firing of this kiln for two hours is comparable—in energy consumed and effluents produced—to a car running at 70 m.p.h. for one hour or a 707 aircraft at cruising speed for three seconds."[9]

"Save that Oil. One of the topics that comes up for discussion periodically, especially in

51. Smoke from chimney during the early stage of an oil firing. (*Ron Moroni*)

light of the voluminous rhetoric about oil imports and oil prices, is why don't we stop wasting oil and reuse this precious commodity? In many other parts of the world oil that is drained from the crankcase of a car is sold to companies that re-refine the oil and sell it again.

"Until 1965, re-refined oil was common in the U.S., too. In that year, however, Congress repealed the excise tax which allowed the major oil companies to cut into the re-refiner's price advantage, and the Federal Trade Commission ruled that re-refiners had to label their products 'previously used oil.' The result of these and other government regulations was the reduction in the number of re-refining companies in the U.S. from 160 to 40 or so today.

"The experts report that approximately 370 million gallons of used oil are probably dumped in this country every year, oil that could be re-refined and put to good use. The Environmental Protection Agency adds that the dumping of oil is causing some problems in sewage treatment facilities in various cities in the U.S. Nevertheless, President Ford and the Congress pay relatively little attention to the problem, conspicuous oil consumption continues and millions of gallons of potentially useful oil are dumped yearly."[10]

Excerpt from "Letters" in *Studio Potter:* "Portions of the article ["Fired Free"] by Mr. Parks were helpful concerning the use of waste oil as a kiln fuel . . . but, *Hold it*!!! Let's not get carried away. . . .

"Mr. Parks' strongest point in his case for using this fuel is its 'economy.' Yes, if the potter doesn't mind a very dirty and heavy fuel which involves time, materials and energy to gather, clean, store and use, money can be saved. However, the time and energy may be better spent in other areas of the craft. Also, the savings in fuel costs may not make up for the deterioration of kiln bricks, furniture and the percentage of fired ware caused by the *vapor glaze, sulfur flaws* and *fire flashing* common to the use of the fuel.

"On the other hand, most people do not consider the pollution of our atmosphere with deadly toxic chemicals as being ecological. Mr. Parks should know that toxic pollutants result from the combustion of waste oil when the original lubrication products contain the normal additives of *chlorine, lead, sulfur, barium, chrome, selenium* and various other chemical compounds. Lubrication oil manufacturers use quantities of these chemicals and others, such as *tellurium, zinc, calcium, magnesium, sodium* and *tin* in their products. These all vaporize in the combustion of the fuel and those which do not end up in our air in toxic form, end up vapor-glazing the bricks, furniture and ware of the kiln, or, as is the case with sulfur, they bloat, pit, bubble and scab the glaze surface of a percentage of each firing.

". . . With time and the general exchange of information among potters using this fuel, the potential of automotive waste oil as a kiln fuel will be realized."[11]

My reply: ". . . I confess I do admire vapor glazing and fire flashing on my pots. . . .

"I also admit ignorance as to why you lose a percentage of each firing to bloating, pitting, etc. If it is sulfur, I cannot understand why Texan drainoil has more than Nevadan. To be straight with you, I just have not had those problems!

". . . The firing of pottery has its ecological price tage [sic] be it strip-mining coal to generate electricity, burying atomic wastes after making electricity, disrupting caribou migration with natural gas pipelines or burning waste drainoil. I don't yet believe that the most visible transgression is necessarily the costliest to our habitat. Is it sounder ecologically to allow drainoil to be poured into the ground or to burn it in a kiln? What is our ecological cost/potter?

"Sniffing automobile exhaust is horrible for our health, but that fact doesn't stop us from driving. Electric kilns should be fired only in a well-ventilated room. Fumes. 'Deadly toxic chemicals.' I have never met a salt-glazing potter who doesn't carry a spot of guilt in his heart or on his lungs.

"I agree we do need 'time and a general exchange of information' on the subject of drainoil firing. In the meanwhile stand upwind while you're firing. Or carry a canary...."[12]

Below is an analysis of a sample of my drainoil, and for comparison an analysis of a native earthenware I have been using for over ten years—and finally, an analysis of a bowl of cornflakes. The chemicals referred to in the letter above are in italics. All amounts listed are in parts/million.

Drainoil[13]

iron	50.	*lead*	500.+
copper	18.	*tin*	5.
chrome	7.	silica	5.
aluminum	7.		

Earthenware Clay[14]

iron	29,000.	nickel	60.
copper	70.	rubidium	100.
lead	320.	strontium	140.
silver	810.	*barium*	1,700.
zinc	350.	titanium	2,400.
cadmium	40.	zirconium	260.
arsenic	130.	manganese	370.
antimony	50.	yttrium	100.
cobalt	40.		

Enriched Cornflakes[15]

iron	14.	*magnesium*	160.
copper	.6–.8	*calcium*	170.
chrome	.04	phosphorus	450.
manganese	1.5	potassium	1,200.
zinc	18.2	*sodium*	100,050.

Organic Gardening and Farming, May 1978: "How Safe Is Newsprint as Mulch? Several years ago the Connecticut Agricultural Station released a report: 'Lead in Paper—A Potential Source of Food Contamination.' This paper cited the lead content of newspaper at 69 parts per million. But food wrappings that come in contact with bakery confections were rated at 10,125 parts per million! Candy bar wrappers contain 7,125 p.p.m., while bread inner liners stand at 6,125 p.p.m."

From this final quote you might reasonably conclude that trash burning is more threatening than kiln firing. But these are just random sherds of evidence. The search for more is not facetious: these issues affect our longevity and livelihood. Because the proper place for a potter is in his studio, each of us must hurry up and settle on a working, ecologically sound compromise. It need not be final.

I find electricity to be a miraculous source of energy for running motors and lighting rooms. I feel guilty heating with it. Wood, gas, and oil are merely small-scale polluters when burned in kilns scattered across the country. A healthy earth can heal small wounds. Firing with drainoil makes use of one of society's waste products. Our majority's obsession with the private automobile (like the individual's right to bear arms) is defended with a constitutional fervor. Whether we like it or not, I believe drainoil will be with us forever. The secondary energy sources needed to collect and combust it are very low. Periodically I check the health of the vegetation downwind from the kiln. I always stand upwind when firing.

Safety

Though fire is inherently dangerous, a kiln has to be one of the safest structures to restrain it. Years ago I approached a local fire chief in California inquiring about regulations before building a kiln in my backyard of his jurisdiction. He looked skeptical. "Have you constructed one before?"

"Yes."

"Well, then you should know the purpose of a ceramic kiln is to contain heat. If you build it right, it's no danger to anybody."

This relaxed attitude from officials is rare.

Some precautions should be made for personal and structural fire safety. With an oil kiln the system from storage tank to burner must be examined with an eye for potential accidents. Fortunately the liquid fuels burned in kilns have relatively high flash points. A lighted cigarette can be extinguished in a cup of diesel, though the practice is not recommended. Difficulty in igniting drainoil, the annoyance in the early firing, is a reassuring safety feature.

A reasonable nightmare for a potter who

52. Double oil burner setup on a 125-cubic-foot kiln: (a) drainoil supply line, insulated automotive heater hose; (b) diesel supply line, heater hose; (c) water supply line; (d) steel pipes which have had their interiors braized closed, installed to support the supply system; (e) air-control valve; (f) blower.

fires with gas is that a leaky pipe or faulty burner fills his kiln and studio with unburned vapors. The dream ends with a cigarette or an electrical spark lighting the bomb. In a similar drama with oil, he returns to witness a burning oil slick, slowly flowing out from the kiln. I have watched it twice.

The plots were the same and worth retelling. A student signed up to fire a kiln through the night. The schedule called for increasing fuel every twenty minutes. He forgot at twenty after the hour, so at twenty of he turned the valve twice as far to compensate. The firebox was not hot enough to vaporize this volume of oil. It flowed in and pooled on the floor. Because of insufficient combustion a ridge of clinker built up directly in front of the burner tip, damming the flow of excess oil. With only its surface vapors aflame, the liquid reversed direction and seeped back out saturating the ground around the burner. Above the fire were the fuel lines.

The student was out of sight. An unrecorded amount of time elapsed before he returned to the kiln. By then flames were licking up the kiln wall and being fed by the fuel hoses which had burned free and dropped to the ground. He rushed to find a bucket of sand and threw it on the base of the fire. When this did not extinguish the blaze, several more bucketsful were tossed in. The flames remained out of control. Another student awakened and came to help. First, he turned off the fuel valves at both tanks, then filled the buckets with sand, and the two students quickly smothered the fire.

The losses in each case were confined to several yards of heater hose and an ungauged amount of oil. The kilns continued firing a little behind schedule. Damage was minimal because: (1) there was no brush nor other flammables in the immediate vicinity; (2) the oil storage tanks were away from the kiln and uphill so that the fire did not flow under and engulf them; (3) the second student thought quickly—first turn off the oil and then throw sand on the fire.

Accidents such as these can be averted if automatic, heat-sensitive valves (Fire-o-matic) are installed on the oil pipes adjacent to the kiln. A well-insulated kiln should be no more than 200° F. (93° C.) on the outside surface. These valves are rated to interrupt the fuel supply when excessive heat reaches them (between 300° F. [148° C.]–400° F. [204° C.]). To further insure safety, rigid steel pipe can be used exclusively for the supply line from the storage tanks to the burners. I continue to use automotive heater hose because of its flexibility and the economy in moving a single burner system from kiln to kiln. For safety, with each new group of students, I repeat my stories.

If you anticipate an inspector visiting your studio, do not guess—check with your local

53. Sixty-cubic-foot kiln fired with two burners on propane, diesel, and drainoil. Studio of Jere Lykins. (*Jere Lykins*)

fire and building departments for specific requirements before installing an oil burner system. When your kiln is in the country where there are no enforced guidelines, maximum caution dictates:

—Locate oil tanks distant from the kiln (ten feet or more) and preferably uphill. If the kiln is inside, have the storage outside.
—Lay the bricks in the floor of the firebox with a moderate slant toward the interior of the kiln to help keep excess oil inside. If clinkers form during a firing, be sure to knock them loose.
—Install only steel or copper pipe in close proximity to the kiln (at least 18 inches of clearance).
—Place heat-sensitive valves on the supply line (between 12 to 18 inches from the kiln). If heater hose is used for part of the line, attach valve where the hose joins the metal pipe.
—Allow no combustibles other than the essential fuel to be in the neighborhood of the kiln.

—Stock a generous supply of sand or loose dirt with buckets and shovels close by, and/or purchase fire extinguishers (type B, C).

Aesthetics

Discussing beauty and drainoil in the same paragraph is necessary. I suggest the irony because I have come to the conclusion that the same clay and glazes which I have fired with gas have new life, richness, vigor (beauty) when fired with drainoil. Of course there is a range of attributes which come to be expected with any fuel: the oxidized purity of unblemished clay from an electric kiln; the scattered blush of ash on the shoulder of a wood-fired jug. But it is the buttery glow in glazes and the warm vapor flashes on clay fired with drainoil that makes it my aesthetic choice (Plate 8). This is a gift from our cultural obsession, well-traveled, jeweled with contaminants (worn down to parts per million): thrown bearings, loose piston rings, leaded gasoline, and S.T.P.

Each barrel is a little different depending on its origin. Airports offer cleaner oil than truck stops. Lots of room for accidents.

The golfer Gary Player said, after winning two consecutive major tournaments, "It's amazing what good luck I have when I practice all the time." The same is partially true for a potter. Experience, knowledge, and hard work assure a high level of consistency in fired results. This is par for the ceramic industry. But in my kilns I expect fire to be more than a means to a predictable end. Fire is invoked as a medium, accepted as a partner in the process. As in any joint venture one principal may dominate the other. When this happens to be the fire in the kiln, the result is labeled an "accident." Some potters are more prone to lucky ones than others. The serendipity which I enjoy with drainoil other potters indulge in with raku and salt glazing.

A scale I constructed (Fig. 54) illustrates the level of surface enrichment that can be expected from different fuels.

Coincidentally you can also speculate as your eye rises on the scale, that the chance of predicting or reproducing the results will decline. Accidents do happen.

"Art is the one thing we cannot make"
—DeKooning.

OIL BURNERS

To fire with oil is not an irrevocable decision. Oil burners will fit in place of gas burners for initial, trial firings. One easy way to experiment with drainoil is to temporarily rig a pipe over your gas burner and drip oil into the gas flame. Adjust the air up to compensate. This enriched gas firing gives some added free Btu's without committing yourself to a major system change.

The choice of which particular oil burner to install is decided on the basis of answers to practical questions like: "What grades of oil will it burn?" "Does it require a blower?" "How much smoke is inevitable?" "What does it cost?" "Can I construct it?"

The following are descriptions of basic types of burners frequently used on oil kilns. Outlined first are the ones I have firsthand knowledge of from firing with them. The others have been recommended by potters who fire regularly with them. All were designed to fire with diesel: most can optionally burn drainoil in the later stages of firing.

Weed Burner

My first oil firings were with two diesel weed burners (Aeroil #13 K-S) purchased secondhand from a blacksmith in Elko. The ware was single-fired raku. These kilns were small, four- to eight-cubic-foot cross drafts with a double back flame pattern. Fire was introduced under the door, shot under the floor, then up and back through the ware until it finally vented out the top of the door. A single burner fired a kiln loaded with raw glazed vessels to cone 04 in three hours on ten gallons of diesel. This much fuel was consumed because these burners can operate at only one setting, full blast. To regu-

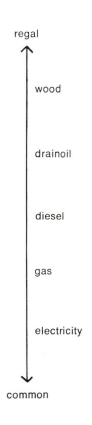

54. Scale of fuels.

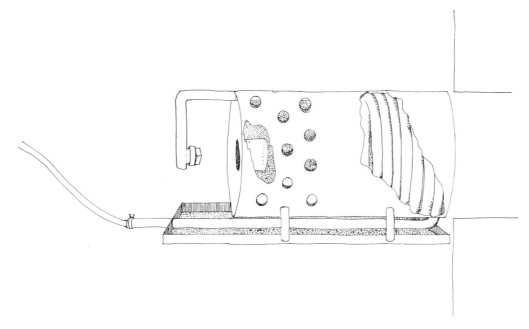

55. Oil weed burner, cutaway drawing. (*Margaret Norman*)

late a gradual rise in temperature, when the burner was lit, it was placed two feet away from the kiln so that only a yellow tip of flame licked into the opening of the port. Then periodically the burner was inched closer.

The weed burner was fueled from a twenty-gallon pressurized oil tank with a built-in hand pump. Before igniting the burner a needle valve on the line was opened allowing one-fourth inch of diesel to collect in the bottom tray. A rag was partially submerged in the oil and lit. The heat from the burning wick raised the temperature of the surrounding oil, and in minutes the vapors were on fire over the entire surface of the tray. These flames played on the bottom of the coils above, transferring heat to the oil inside, initially expanding the liquid and then vaporizing it. This pressurized oil vapor was expelled from an orifice at the rear of the burner and ignited as it passed over the flaming tray, through the center of the coils. The valve was then opened all the way so that the pressure in the storage tank could push a steady supply of diesel into the heated coils to continue the vaporization.

The absence of control over the flame size which resulted in excessive fuel consumption was the main disadvantage of the system. Another problem developed. After repeated firings the intense heat reflecting back from the firebox prematurely burned vapors still inside the coils. Gradually an internal carbon deposit formed that eventually plugged the coils. I returned the burners to the blacksmith who showed me how to burn this blockage out by filling the coils with oxygen and applying a torch to the outside. Unfortunately, after two or three subsequent cleansings, spots in the metal coil deteriorated into holes.

My final objection to weed burners was my initial impression—they sound like a jet taxiing for takeoff. I still have not thrown them away. They are clean burning, and could be economical if used occasionally for the rapid raku firing of bisqued pieces.

Drip-Feed Pipe Burner

To fire a larger stoneware kiln, I decided to fabricate two diesel burners suggested by my former teacher, Paul Soldner. The simplicity of design was compelling. From his drawing these burners looked as though they would not clog and, even with a blower, should fire with minimal noise.

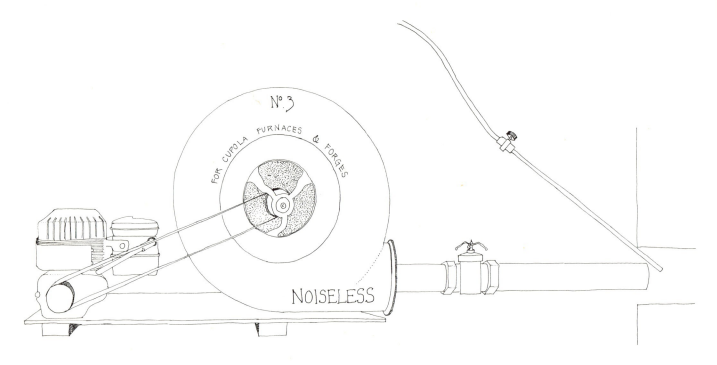

56. Drip-feed pipe burner. (*Margaret Norman*)

Before the blower was attached, the burners operated on the same principle as the vaporizing tray of the weed burner. Oil dripped from the top pipe onto a floor brick in the burner port where it pooled. A newspaper was used to torch it. As the host brick heated, more oil could be introduced. The hotter the brick, the quicker fuel transformed to vapor and burned.

The exact length of time before a blower is needed depends on the natural draught of the kiln, which in turn varies with wind conditions, barometric pressure, etc. I figure when a fire looks deficient in oxygen, then I compensate with a blower.

It was eight hours into the maiden firing when I noted that I had increased the fuel several partial turns with no noticeable rise in temperature. To cut down on the smoke, I added air.

A neighbor who has a museum of mining relics donated the rusty forge blower (B. F. Sturtevant, #3 Noiseless, patent 1887). To this antique I hitched a new, three-horsepower gasoline engine (Briggs & Stratton); a system that was far from "noiseless," but for a change sounded more like a motorbike than an aircraft. When electricity reached Tuscarora a few years later, I retired the forge blower and bought a secondhand vacuum cleaner, not as old nor quite as loud. Today I use a commercial blower (Clements-Cadillac; model HP3; one-horsepower; 27,000 lineal feet per minute).

The gate valve on the air pipe gave me control over the volume of air blowing into the firebox. Too much air would cool down the puddling brick, retard vaporization, and possibly blow out the fire. Periodically the air and oil were alternately increased until the air was on full. At this point the diesel was adjusted to provide a steady, clean atmosphere throughout the kiln. Kneeling down I could look into the burner port and see that in a crude way the blast of air was atomizing the stream of oil. A shower of oil droplets was being blown into a red-hot firebox.

The first firing was long and slow up to cone 1. A new fuel is intimidating. I did not know what I was doing and my old teacher was a thousand miles away. Frequently checking through the peephole, I tried to maintain an interior atmosphere that I was accustomed to seeing in a gas kiln, bright and clean. A pyrometer would have helped. When cone 1 finally softened, I closed the air valve halfway and slid the dampers shut. Twenty minutes later I reversed the procedure, clearing the smoke out of the kiln. When I looked in the peephole, I was unprepared for what I saw. Both cone 1 and cone 5 had melted during "reduction."

In unloading the kiln, looking at the pale clay body, it was obvious that the pieces were only lightly reduced. Still the firing was good for I learned : (1) fire with a rich atmosphere, murky to the extent that the cones are barely visible; (2) reduce with the blower unplugged.

Modified Pipe Burner

After five years of experience and satisfaction firing with a pipe burner, I set about tinkering with the design. The changes were minor but did improve the effectiveness of the original in both the early vaporizing and later atomizing stage.

An ⅛-inch-diameter rod, 2½ inches long, was welded to the bottom of the lip of the oil pipe. In the early stage of firing this led the oil further into the firebox. Since the viscosity of the fuel held it to the rod, the liquid flowed along the full circumference. This action thinned the diesel enough so that it sustained a flame before dripping onto the firebox floor. Quicker vaporization promoted more complete combustion which resulted in less early smoke.

The second modification was to weld a ¾-inch ball bearing on the end of the rod. Exactly half of the ball was ground off so that this flat surface was parallel to the end of the air pipe. After the blower was switched on, this new half-dome functioned as an airfoil forcing the spray of air and the oil droplets into a wide yet deep dispersal pattern. Now the kiln fired cleaner throughout the schedule.

Propane/Oil Combination

Any simple oil vaporizing system operating below red heat produces some smoke. The addition of the drip rod to the modified pipe burner was a small improvement. The problem remains that oils will always be inefficient at low temperatures because of their high flash points. If you substitute propane in the beginning, the problem is skirted. A gas, though inferior in Btu's, is easier to control and more efficient than oil in the lower range.

An inexpensive propane weed burner will conveniently slip inside a modified pipe burner if the air pipe is 2⅜ inches i.d. (inside dimension) or larger. After the gas valve is all the way open, oil can be dripped into the flame and then periodically increased. This type of sleeve burner stays in place up to the time a blower is needed.

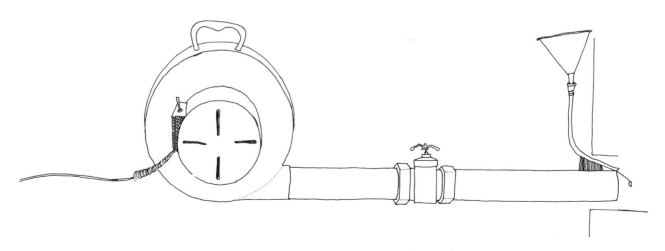

57. Modified pipe burner. (*Margaret Norman*)

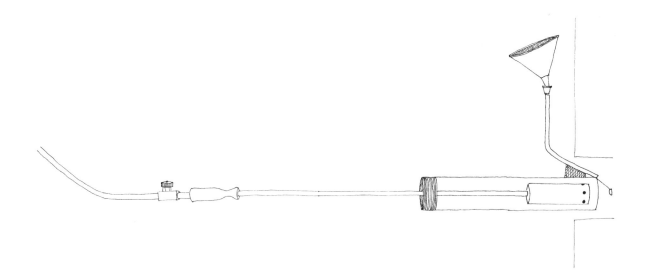

58. Propane/oil combination burner, cutaway drawing. (*Margaret Norman*)

59. Propane/oil combination burner firing with propane. (*Ron Moroni*)

60. Propane/oil combination burner with blower attached, firing with oil. (*Ron Moroni*)

61. Three-chambered kiln. The first chamber is fired with wood, the second with drainoil, and the third reaches earthenware temperature with the heat from the first two chambers. Studio of Peter Dick.

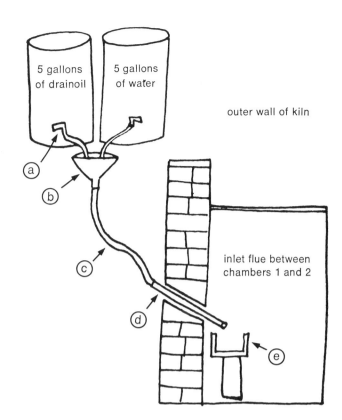

62. Second chamber, showing the drainoil burning system in Peter Dick's kiln: (a) plastic tap; (b) metal funnel; (c) garden hose; (d) metal pipe; (e) short section of channel iron sitting on a brick. "This very crude system will only work in a '2' or subsequent chamber. The burner plate must be very hot as must the primary air. We get a perfectly clean burn and excellent control of reduction/oxidation and plenty of rise to 1300° C." (*Katy Hertel*)

Wood/Oil Combination

Wood can also be burned as the initial heat source. When the firebox reaches red heat you place an oil burner in the stoke hole and complete the cycle. Since a firebox that burns wood needs grates and an ashpit, the kiln must be constructed with this contingency in the plans.

Several potters in England switched from all wood firing to the combination because feeding oil to a kiln is not as laborious as chopping, splitting, and stoking wood—yet the pots still come out with the distinctive ash blush. Wood is smokier than oil, but it is pleasantly scented and generally free. The economic advantage of a wood/drainoil kiln is indisputable. Even here in the high desert there are enough dead willows in the canyons to fire a 50-cubic-foot kiln biweekly. Other fuel is purchased only in the summer when there is worry about flying sparks starting a range fire.

Holaday Burner

The Holaday Burner is named after Inez Holaday who, as far as I know, was the first to use it. The burner was a creation of necessity. She was hired through the mail for her first job

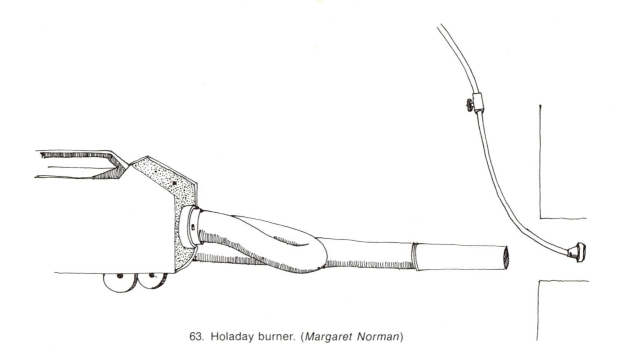

63. Holaday burner. (*Margaret Norman*)

constructing a kiln. When she arrived at the site, she was told, "Here are the firebricks, but there's no money for anything else." Period.

The burner she settled on was not designed but rather it happened; an assemblage of donations from the community—simple and effective. A length of ⅜-inch copper tubing descended from a raised oil barrel into the center of the burner port. A flare fitting was attached to the open end of the tube and this rested on the lip of a propane weed burner. Propane heated the firebox initially. When the gas had been turned on full, oil (diesel or drainoil) was dripped into the flame and periodically increased until the propane tank (five gallons) was empty. At this time the weed burner was removed and replaced by a vacuum-cleaner blower. To control the volume of air the blower was placed three feet back from the kiln and pushed forward as more air was needed.

The force of air blowing around a cone-shaped flare-fitting creates the finest spray of any of these homemade, orificeless, atomizing systems. When the oil reaches the fitting, it is pulled to the interior leading edge where it flies off in a spray of minute droplets.

Some particles of dirt and sand were picked up by the blast of air from the distant blower and, after the firing, were discovered to be glazed in the bottoms of pots. This problem was eventually solved by passing the hat and purchasing a valve for air control.

Stepladder or Louvre Burner

The origin and ancestry of the stepladder or louvre burner is unrecorded. Examples in current use can be found on kilns in England and Japan as well as here in this country. The unique advantage of this burner is that it is the only drip burner that fires without a blower. Since it does rely on natural draft, the design of the kiln is critical. Only an updraft or cross draft with an adequate chimney will pull the volume of oxygen needed for combustion.

As the names suggest, the burner is constructed of a series of steps which the fuel runs down, dripping, vaporizing, and burning as it descends. Most of the designs have a minimum of three steel steps arranged at the mouth of the firebox. These can be welded in place to uprights or positioned temporarily on brick posts.

A small wood or rag bonfire is started directly in front prior to dripping diesel on the plates. As these steps heat up, the oil running down them is adjusted so that its vapors burn or are drafted into the kiln before any liquid

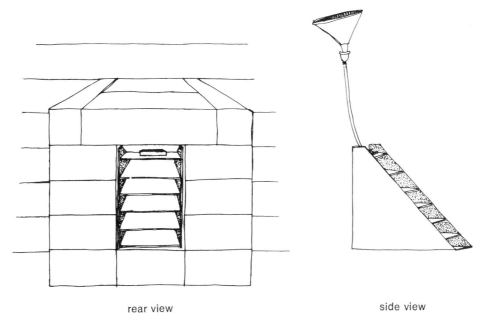

64. Stepladder or louvre burner. (*Margaret Norman*)

reaches the bottom step. Some potters construct an extended firebox to allow more area for the preliminary bonfire, and to accommodate the longer flames.

The louvre system is notoriously smoky up to red heat. The beauty of the setup is that it demands basically only one fuel, oil—no electricity to run a blower, and no propane to burn for warm-up. Drainoil can be the fuel used for the bulk of the firing.

Low-Pressure Orifice Burners

In this category lie a number of burners with different names—Denver, New Zealand, and New Soldner—but all are quite similar in design and performance. Unlike the previous drip-fed burners, which have a ⅜-inch opening for the oil to come out, these may have an orifice as small as 1/32 inch. To maintain the gravity pressure necessary to squirt oil through such a constriction, the storage tank must be raised four to eight feet above the level of the burner.

Another consideration is the distance between the orifice and the burner tip, which is critical if the spray is to come out even and well-patterned. By not welding the oil pipe on at the rear of the burner, this can be adjusted.

Since small orifices sometimes plug from

65. New Zealand burner. The end of the oil supply tube is flattened to approximately 1/32 inch to form an oval orifice. A larger corresponding pattern is formed in the center of the pipe cap (burner tip) by drilling three ⅜-inch holes ½ inch apart and filing to complete the aperture. (*Margaret Norman*)

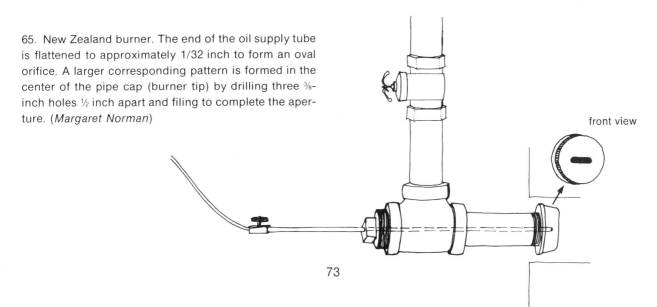

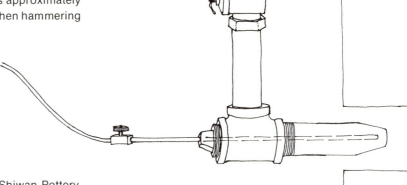

66. New Soldner burner. The orifice is crimped to roughly 1/16 inch in diameter, and the tip of the burner is narrowed to half its original diameter. This reduction can be done either with a standard bell reducer that screws on or by cutting a series of slots approximately 3 inches into the length of the pipe and then hammering to the size desired. (*Margaret Norman*)

67. Low-pressure orifice burner at the Shiwan Pottery, Fushan, The People's Republic of China. According to interpreters, the firings are begun with kerosene. This fuel is used until the firebox is hot enough to sustain combustion of mazut (Bunker C, #6 fuel oil). Notice that the oil supply pipe is embedded in the outer wall of the kiln to preheat this heavy oil.

dirt or sludge, installing a filter between the tank and the burner is recommended. If drainoil is introduced, not only should it be filtered, but it may have to be diluted with a lighter oil or thinned with heat.

Orifice burners have the problem that their lowest efficient setting produces too much heat for the early stage of firing. To solve this the oil pipe can be pushed to a forward position where the fuel drips onto a brick and vaporizes, or one of the combinations (wood or propane) can be incorporated.

After reaching red heat these burners fire clean and fast—too fast, say some potters. Certain glazes may blister and pit unless the firing is slowed down for a heat soaking short of the maturation temperature.

The New Zealand and New Soldner burners have the advantage of being readily assembled with standard pipe fittings. The diameter of the pipe is normally between one and three inches i.d. (inside dimensions), the larger recommended when fewer burners are installed.

SETTING UP A SYSTEM TO BURN DRAINOIL

In order to turn waste oil into fuel, two problems must be overcome—contamination and

THE MODIFIED TUSCARORA DRAINOIL DIESEL COMBINATION BURNER SYSTEM
As Illustrated Here on a One-Burner Downdraft Kiln

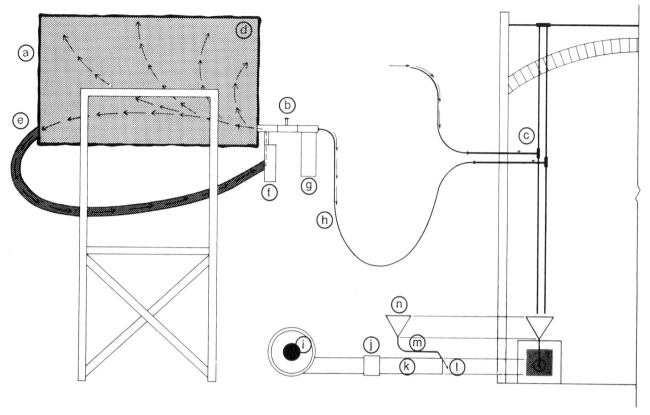

(a) 1" thick insulation (Armstrong Armaflex)
(b) gate valve
(c) needle valves
(d) 55-gallon (or larger) oil drum
(e) oil exit connection
    must be drilled and fabricated
(f) engine block heater 1000 watts
(g) sediment bowl (Wicks Fuel Filter #24389—filter removed)
(h) heater hose (covered with Armaflex Pipe Insulation)
(i) blower (Clements Cadillac HP3)
(j) gate valve
(k) pipe 2 3/8" i.d., 16" long
(l) welding rod, attached to lower lip of oil pipe
(m) oil pipe 3/8" i.d.
(n) funnel

68. Tuscarora diesel/drainoil system. (*Valerie Parks*)

viscosity. By definition drainoil is contaminated. The small particles I consider a bonus; pieces large enough to plug a pipe or a valve are contaminating. Seldom does the trouble originate in the automobile crankcase. It is thoughtlessness at the service station that lands flip-tops and Kleenex in the oil. To prevent these from blocking the oil line I have a policy of straining the oil through 30-mesh screen (window screen or kitchen strainer) each time the oil is transferred from one container to another. This takes place once at the station and again at the storage tank. For a drip burner this is all the purification necessary.

A sediment bowl is installed on the line adjacent to the tank. Since water is heavier than oil, what condenses in the tank settles in the

69. Pumping oil from a 55-gallon transit barrel to a 100-gallon heating tank. (*Ron Moroni*)

bowl. To serve this purpose I bought a Wicks Fuel Filter (#24389) and removed the filter. The gravity pressure of the system is not sufficient to push drainoil through the dense paper nor is such fine filtration required. If you are firing with an orifice burner, an added precaution would be to jury-rig a 60-mesh screen at the exit of the sediment bowl.

The high viscosity of drainoil is a year 'round problem with orifice burners. Mixing in 25 to 50 percent diesel, depending on how cold the weather is, will improve the flow.

With drip burners the sluggishness is a contention only in the winter. I overcome it by preheating the oil and insulating both the tank and the supply line. Automotive parts stores carry a variety of engine block heaters that do the job. A heater with a thermostat will cut the power off when liquid temperature reaches 170° F. (76.6° C.), safely below the flash point.

For insulation I settled on a one-inch-thick flexible pad and tubing (Armstrong-Armaflex) which, though relatively expensive, is easy to cut and glue and withstands adverse weather. By insulating well, less electricity is drawn during the warm-up. My practice is to plug the heater in while the kiln is being loaded, then unplug it when the blower is turned on. At the end of the firing, ten hours later, the remaining oil is still 150° F. (66° C.).

Remember when filling the storage tank, oil expands with heat. Leave room at the top and do not cap it tightly. A 100-gallon barrel is more than adequate storage for most potters (75 gallons of oil fires a 125-cubic-foot kiln). Having an excess in the tank assures steady pressure and an even flow throughout the firing.

For transferring oil from one barrel to another, I keep a heavy fluid and grease pump (Charles SV-55) that is powered with a ½-inch electric drill. The manufacturer states that, for example, it will pump five gallons of SAE-30 per minute. In use I find the chore takes twice as long.

The firings here consume an average of 150 gallons a month; still the city supply exceeds country demand. Some of the backlog is burned in the winter in a commercial waste oil heater (Kutrieb CT 70) to warm the studios.

THE VALUE OF ADDING WATER TO OIL

The function of the sediment bowl is to collect water and prevent it from flowing into the firebox to the exclusion of drainoil. But ironically a little water introduced in the funnel together with the fuel has a beneficial, tonic effect. As a child I was raised with the warning, "Never throw water on an oil fire! It will only make the fire get worse." Of course that is exactly what we are trying to do inside the kiln.

The introduction of a drip-line of water adds some extra oxygen to the fire. More dramatic is

70. Three pipes in the funnel: drainoil, diesel, and water. (*Ron Moroni*)

new Ford and a new Chevrolet. So few details vary that from across the street you cannot tell the difference. Switching a kiln from gas to oil requires making only simple modifications. The gas kiln has too many burner ports. Some of these should be bricked up, and the firebox may need to be enlarged to accept a longer, hotter flame.

The first kiln I converted was a four-burner updraft with flame channels running under the floor. I blocked two ports and placed oil burners in the other two. No problems arose until late in the fourth firing when the bricks around the channels deformed and the floor col-

the spitting and crackling scene in the firebox as the water fries and steams in the hot oil. Visualize water in bacon grease. This violence in the firebox is spattering oil everywhere, breaking down the particle size which in turn speeds vaporization and combustion. No clinkers form. The fuel burns more completely: the kiln fires cleaner.

Usually I start a hesitant drip of water when the firebox has reached red heat, then increase it to about 20 percent of the oil flow. I have heard of potters who use up to 30 or 40 percent water.

THE OIL-FIRED KILN

The differences in design between an oil kiln and a gas kiln are as minor as that between a

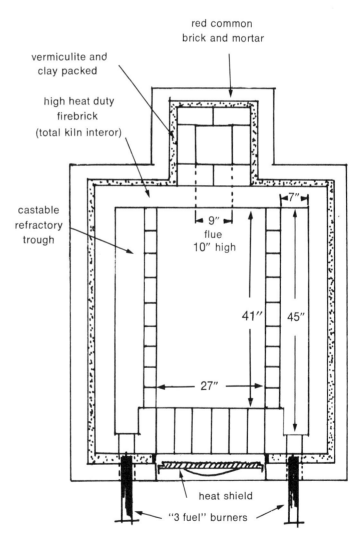

71. Floor plan of 60-cubic-foot oil-fired kiln of Jere Lykins. Big Texas Valley Pottery, Rome, Georgia. (*Jere Lykins*)

lapsed. Oil flames are more intense than gas flames.

When I reconstructed the floor, I left two open channels on opposite sides of the kiln for the flame's passage. (In building subsequent kilns, updraft, cross-draft and downdraft, this has proved to be a satisfactory design.) By making channels a platform was created, 11½ inches high, which served as the first level for loading pots. One side of each channel functioned as a bag-wall. The only drawback in these long, open fireboxes is that an area of potential loading space is lost.

Recently I discovered a bibliography of literature printed by the oil-heating industry written for the maintenance man concerned with installation and repair of domestic and commercial oil burners. Without exception the authors recommend short fireboxes ("combustion chambers") with corbeled bag-walls. They further suggest constructing the bag-wall of insulation brick. Its surface heats more rapidly than hard firebricks, which tend to absorb and transfer heat away from the surface. The idea is to have atomized oil strike a superheated bag-wall where it quickly vaporizes and combusts. A corbeled design creates a turbulence and also radiates more heat back into the flame.

Home heating specialists desire a clean, short flame concentrating heat in the combustion chamber, while potters look for a soft, long flame wafting through the kiln. Too short a flame leaves us with melted bag-walls; too long a flame fills the kiln yard with smoke. The wisdom of industry should not be ignored.

The compromise is a firebox long enough to prevent destruction, but as short as possible to

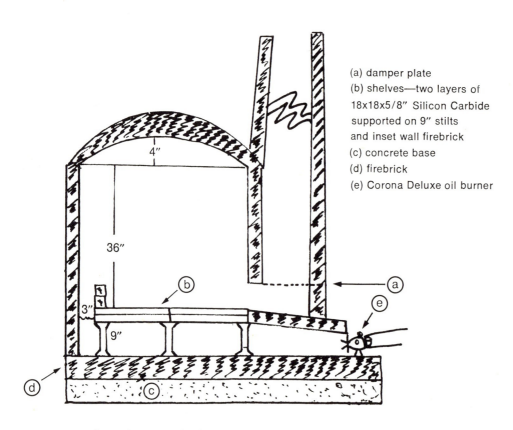

(a) damper plate
(b) shelves—two layers of 18x18x5/8" Silicon Carbide supported on 9" stilts and inset wall firebrick
(c) concrete base
(d) firebrick
(e) Corona Deluxe oil burner

Approximate Interior Dimensions

  chamber—40x40x36" (height to the arch base)
  arch—4" rise at the center
  stack—6" square by 14'
  firebox—24" long, 9" wide at chamber

72. Toenshiki kiln, Japanese downdraft, sideloading oil-firing kiln. Though I have had no success with firing with oil underneath the floor in a kiln, Burt Cohen wrote that this is a popular design in Japan and is fired with a single, high-pressure, commercial burner. (*Burt Cohen*)

promote combustion, and to provide optimum loading space. Begin by building a large one. It is easy with more bricks to decrease the area of the firebox. I recommend a generous ratio of 3:1 (floor loading area to firebox).

In layout I favor the long, narrow box with a drip burner and the short, wide one with an orifice burner. The latter has a broader spray pattern. An exception to the rule is the Holaday burner which, though a drip burner in design, throws a large-diameter atomized pattern. I fired one successfully in a small kiln with a bag-wall less than 12 inches from the burner tip.

When firing with gas, the old kiln rule was that the more burners you stuck in the more likely the kiln was to heat evenly. Firing with oil, multiple burners are redundant. I think of the analogy of a single firebox on a wood kiln, but instead of stoking wood I am squirting oil. One oil burner adequately feeds the fire in kilns up to 50 cubic feet; two burners up to at least 125 cubic feet.

The classic oil flame is orange, long, and bushy. Bag-wall and damper adjustments push or pull it where it is needed. In a downdraft, opening the damper or lowering the bag-wall will build temperature in the bottom of the kiln; closing the damper or raising the bag-wall will hold heat in the top. To correct an updraft firing cooler in the bottom, narrow the damper opening or lower the bag-wall. If it is hotter in the bottom, do the opposite.

AN IDEALIZED FIRING SCHEDULE

The underlying assumption is that most potters have previously learned how to fire with a gas kiln. The scheme and pitfalls are familiar. We understand: no two kilns fire identically; one kiln may not fire the same twice in a row; each firing varies according to how it is packed, what the weather is like outside, what burners are used, who watches the kiln, and many unrecorded nuances. This schedule is a synopsis of an oil firing when everything goes well.

Single-firing requires treating the event as a bisque firing up to red heat, then as a glaze firing. If you hear a piece explode, it is wise to stop firing and unload the sherds before they become glazed appendages on surrounding pots. Because this is a boring extra step, I always fire slowly.

The commitment to burning a liquid fuel makes you shift your thinking. An oil kiln needs more attention in the early hours: the liquid is temperamental igniting and slow to red heat. Later in the schedule, all those Btu's may melt the cones faster than you are accustomed to seeing. On occasion I have pulled a peephole brick and witnessed a cone gradually lie down.

The following outline comes out of my experience using modified pipe burners with drainoil as the major fuel and diesel as the starter. Propane or wood may be substituted for diesel on a parallel basis to build the gradual rise to dull red heat. If different burners are used, the procedures may vary slightly, but the principles remain the same.

Reduction with drainoil is not as simple as I would like it to be. In the past when I fired all the way with diesel, the regime I settled on was basic. Reduce—unplug blower and shut damper for twenty minutes. The problem with drainoil under this program is that it cools too rapidly, pools, seeps, and soon floods ominously outside the kiln. I am not proud of doing it, but for the present I revert to diesel during each reduction. This revisionism is not expensive in diesel terms, but it is a small compromise.

Anytime during the firing a clinker may start forming in the firebox. If it is ignored, a large accumulation can build and seriously restrict the flame passage. It develops when two things coincide—*excessive* fuel is blown into a *cool* firebox. Instead of vaporizing, the unburned oil grows into a formidable little hill of carbon. This can usually be broken up by poking with a metal rod. After it is knocked loose, the oil should be adjusted down or the air up to inhibit another one from forming. Check for secondary air that might be cooling the firebox by leaking in around the burner or through cracks in the wall.

Firing Schedule

Six-hour candle—Light a paper or rag fire in the burner port directly in front of your burner. Turn the diesel on so that it will begin dripping (at a heartbeat rate) into this bonfire. Stay by the valve until the flame is adjusted, slow and steady. During this preheating, check intermittently to be sure that the oil is still burning. Unlike unburned gas which will dissipate in the wind, unburned oil will run between bricks, seep into the subfloor and finally come out around the base of your kiln. Later in the firing this excess will fume and smoke.

First to eighth hour—After six hours of candling, begin to periodically increase the diesel. I favor a twenty-minute interval because it allows me enough time to also work on other projects around the studio. The idea is to institute a very gradual rise in temperature. Avoid flooding the bricks with a pool of oil larger than an Eisenhower dollar.

Eighth to twelfth hour—Switch the blower on and open the air to its lowest setting, *i.e.*, until there is a change in the flame's configuration. With a gate valve this allows approximately a ¼-inch air passage. Every twenty minutes alternately increase the air and oil. Chimney smoke should reflect this change from relatively clear to mildly smoky. Occasionally, from the rising efficiency of the hot firebox, the kiln clears itself. So when it should be time to add air, the kiln is already burning clean. Deviate and increase the oil instead. *The steady heat rise is more important than the schedule.* Continue alternating until air is on full. Caution: Too much air too quickly can blow a flame out; too little will stall the temperature climb.

Twelfth to fifteenth hour—With luck the lower

73. Tuscarora Pottery School kiln yard. Raku kilns in foreground. All kilns are fired with drainoil.

shelves have a hazy glow. It is the time to start introducing a drip of drainoil. During this period, as drainoil is gradually increased, diesel is gradually phased out. When the force of the blower is hurling a storm of oil droplets deep into the firebox, there is no longer a need to see, or worry about regulating, the size of the oil puddle. Brick up around the outside of the burner port to block out secondary air which cools the walls of the firebox and retards vaporization. Aluminum foil is my choice for plugging irregular-shaped openings adjacent to the round burner.

Fifteenth hour—Cone 1 down. If the cone does not want to fall, work at tuning the oil valves until the kiln maintains a murky atmosphere where the cone pad is barely visible. Be patient.

Sixteenth hour—Cone 5 down.

Seventeenth hour—Cone 8 down.

Eighteenth hour—Cone 10 down. Kiln off.

In such a typical firing a 50-cubic-foot kiln will consume 15 gallons of diesel and 35 gallons of drainoil; a 125-cubic-foot kiln, 15 gallons of diesel and 75 gallons of drainoil.

CHAPTER 6

Conclusion: The Kiln... and the Countryside

HOW TO BUILD A DIRT-CHEAP KILN

"That's one small step for man...ah...one giant leap for mankind"—Neil Armstrong, July 16, 1969, 10:56 P.M.

There is excited talk among some potters these days about the use of spaceage materials to replace bricks in the building of kilns. We have witnessed the development of kaolin fibers that can be spun, woven, braided, and tied. When they are used to line a kiln, according to the manufacturers, the thermal qualities are "x" times more effective than standard brick insulation. A few potters argue passionately that in the near future all studios should be equipped with super-efficient, soft, upholstered kilns.

What I would like to outline here is a giant step backward—how to use dirt in building your kiln. The ground we walk on, a rough mixture of loam, sand, and clay, can be an excellent insulator for kilns so long as the earth is protected from heat high enough to vitrify or melt it.

Traditionally, a studio potter's kiln is constructed with at least two layers of high temperature insulation, *i.e.*, two walls of firebricks or one wall firebricks and the other of insulation bricks. What I propose is substituting a wall of common dirt in place of the outside bricks; very little if any insulating value is lost and there accrues a remarkable saving in dollars.

Dirt is cheap, easily obtained, and no special skills are needed to work with it. Its disadvantage, in this application, is that it requires hard physical labor. Here again is the classic quandary of time versus money. "Is it worth it? Would you rather work to make the cash to buy the bricks or would you rather work making the bricks?"

Necessity pushed me to look at dirt as a kiln-building material. During a summer workshop that was to have emphasized salt firing, most of the brick pile disappeared quickly into three student-built raku kilns. Calculating very closely, I estimated that there were barely enough bricks remaining for a 20-cubic-foot salt kiln, one layer thick. Time was too short to order more bricks. Looking around for alternatives, all I could see were rocks and dirt. The unevenness of rocks posed a technical problem that, not being a stone mason, to overcome would have involved an added expense for lots of cement.

The earthen shell was formed after first laying up the interior course of firebricks (Fig. 75). A 12-inch-high board was secured, six inches away from the base of the wall. Into the space I packed a damp mixture of local clay and gravel. This particular random mix was chosen only because a pile happened to be in the kiln yard.

After the first course was filled and tamped, the wooden form was raised and the process repeated until the wall was level with the base

74. Making a dirt brick.

75. Construction of a monobloc earthen shell.

76. Laying an adobe brick arch.

of the arch. For variety, the earthen arch was laid with handmade, adobe-like bricks (Fig. 76). The same gravelly clay was rammed into a long, rectangular loaf form and cut into convenient and roughly equal-sized bricks. These were then placed in rows on top of the arch.

There was nothing precious about the kiln. Structural chances were taken because it was intended to stand for only one month, but the idea was not abandoned at the end of the summer. Earth had proved to be good, cheap insulation. In dismantling the kiln the earthen surface facing the firebricks appeared to have a low bisque while the outside was unchanged. Halfway through the earth you could see small air pockets where organic material had been. This kiln had fired as rapidly as a similar-sized, double-wall firebrick kiln and the outside surface was actually cooler to touch.

The next kiln built with earth was fired regularly for three years, and it demonstrated the weakness of monobloc walls. Long random cracks that appeared in the early firings opened up and widened with each heating and cooling cycle. Chinking helped to repair the loss of insulating value, but finally these rents threatened to collapse the structure.

By the time I came to rebuilding, I had bought a hand-operated, earth-block press (Cinva-Ram). These inexpensive tools have been used extensively by the Peace Corps in underdeveloped countries to produce solid earthen bricks for construction. The money I saved on the next kiln, by using these bricks in place of firebricks on the outside wall, more than compensated for the purchase price of the machine. All my subsequent kilns have been constructed similarly and I have gotten further use out of the machine by using the blocks for the walls of my studio.

Building a kiln out of small modular units, such as these, minimized the problem of cracking that had developed in the monobloc walls. Expansion and contraction during the heating and cooling cycles were accommodated by the minute spaces defining the individual bricks. Since 4,000 pounds of pressure comes to bear through leverage of the machine, it is estimated that the blocks are at least twice as strong as manually formed equivalents. This compression makes an outside wall more resistant to the erosion of rain and wind. Also, the uniformity of size is appreciated when you begin laying the walls.

Finding a suitable earth mix may require some trial-and-error experimenting. I started by using backyard soil that was left around after digging the foundations for a studio. I have continued to use similar ground because I have had no troubles.

The simplest way to begin is to press a few test bricks out of any handy, local dirt. Let them dry. Any modifications are on the same principle that a clay body is adjusted. If the bricks are crumbly and difficult to handle, add clay (or a more clayey soil) to the next batch. On the other hand, if the bricks warp or crack, add sand. The workable range is quite broad with adjustments made in shovelsful. To cut down on the number of experiments, start with a source of soil that promises to be abundant and consistent. Each brick will take about 17 pounds of earth, so 500 bricks will use up four and a quarter tons of loose ground.

Even when building with pressed blocks made of well-balanced soil, the exposed surfaces may eventually show deterioration from weather. If a freezing night follows a rain, the moisture will expand the earth and crumble it, leaving it vulnerable to erosion. This need not happen. A kiln can be built indoors or a shed can be built to shelter it. A less expensive alternative is to "stabilize" the earth, *i.e.*, lower its porosity.

Contractors who use earth in building homes recommend adding 5 to 15 percent emulsified asphalt to the wet mix prior to pressing—the more asphalt the lower the absorption. Unfortunately the final strength decreases in direct proportion to the amount of additive. I was skeptical of using this emulsion for another reason—the untested suspicion that the material would smoke and fume and possibly ignite.

Government publications on this subject go on to suggest three other possibilities: (1) add five to ten percent Portland cement to the earth mix; (2) paint the outside surface of the dry blocks with clear liquid silicone; (3) coat the exterior of the structure with stucco.

I have been forced to use all three. The cement improved the handling strength of my blocks, but did nothing to prevent moisture from penetrating and freezing. Though a generous application of silicone was good in waterproofing the walls, it proved ineffective on the arch. So I capped the kilns with a thin application of stucco.

The weather in this part of the country hits all extremes: 100° F. in the summer, −20° F. in the winter; a little rain, a lot of snow, and the wind blows. If your kiln is fired in a more moderate clime, either the cement or the silicone alone should give adequate protection. Where rains are heavy and frequent, the silicone and stucco combination would be advisable, but both of these can be applied later once erosion has proved to be a problem. There is no reason to be overly cautious in the beginning. Earthen blocks are not tied into the insulating core of the kiln. The first evidence of deterioration will be on the arch where, if necessary, the blocks are easy to replace.

The Cinva-Ram Block Press is manufactured in Bogotá, Colombia, and designed to be operated by unskilled labor anywhere in the world. After two blocks you should have complete knowledge of its mechanics and operating procedure. A gifted, mechanically inclined potter with welding equipment could even make his own press. I have heard tales of peasants in Belize producing 500 blocks per day and read of workers on Taiwan averaging 700. Here my crews are unsalaried, drafted locally—students, adolescents, and vacationing city friends. All have soft hands. If 400 blocks come out one day, none are produced for the next two. Monotony and blisters. I have learned that when the daily goal is only 200, an American crew will return to the press several days in a row. Three workers can make the quota in six hours; four can do the same in only four hours.

The most efficient machine to dig and pile up a large volume of loose dirt is a backhoe. If one is not available, a garden Rototiller is a distant second. If a pick and shovel is the highest level of technology on hand, add two people to keep production up.

In order to form well-compressed blocks, the dirt needs to be free of clods and large stones. A wooden frame covered with ¼-inch hard-

77. Sifting dirt. (*Ron Moroni*)

ware cloth will serve as a screen; the dimensions of it depend on the number in your crew and their goals. The screen illustrated (Fig. 77) was adequate for a demonstration, but twice that size would be more realistic for production.

The routine that works well with Tuscarora dirt is to throw eleven shovelsful of screened earth, to one of Portland cement, into a deep wheelbarrow (Fig. 78). Mix thoroughly with a hoe until the gray streaks of cement have disappeared. Pour water in slowly and continue the mixing. This size batch needs two quarts of water—more or less depending on how dry the ground is (Fig. 79). The test for "enough water" is to grab a handful of ingredients and squeeze; it should just barely stay together as a ball when you open your hand (Fig. 80). Insufficient water produces a flaky block that will crumble when you attempt to lift it; excessive water gives you one that deforms when handled.

Shovel the damp mixture from the wheelbarrow into the Cinva-Ram hopper (Fig. 81). Compress slightly with your fingers, particu-

78. Combining dirt and cement. (*Ron Moroni*)

79. Final hoeing after water has been added. (*Ron Moroni*)

80. Testing the consistency of the batch. (*Ron Moroni*)

81. Loading the hopper. (*Ron Moroni*)

82. Beginning the compression stroke. (*Ron Moroni*)

83. Completing compression. (*Ron Moroni*)

84. Block emerges. (*Ron Moroni*)

85. Removing the block. (*Ron Moroni*)

larly at the corners. Level it and swing the lid into place (Fig. 82). The handle is at 45°. Raise it to 90°, click the release switch at the base of the handle and then continue the motion to 180° for compression (Fig. 83).

One healthy, average-size person should be able to complete the stroke—with effort. If the pull is easy, the brick will be weak. More dirt is needed in the hopper. The other extreme comes when the weight of two persons is needed to force the handle down. This is proof of too much dirt and will sometimes produce bricks with an irregular top. Continued overload is one sure way to break the machine.

Return the handle to its original 45° position. Swing the lid to the side and then push the handle down to 0°. This forces the new block to rise up out of the hopper, ready to be removed (Fig. 84).

You can avoid damaging the corners of the fresh block if you grasp it with your palms on opposite ends and press in slightly as you lift up (Fig. 85).

The blocks should be stored on a flat surface, "cured," and protected from freezing until completely dry (Fig. 86). I pile them one on top of another to a height of ten or twelve with no distortion to the blocks on the bottom. Cement products must be cured —kept damp for at least three days (two weeks, if possible) to en-

86. The beginning of a stack. (*Ron Moroni*)

able the material to develop maximum strength. The humidity can be maintained by either wrapping the pile in plastic or covering it with burlap and spraying it daily. While the blocks are still moist, they should not be allowed to freeze as this will prevent the cement from setting.

After they are cured, the pile should be restacked in a looser arrangement to allow more circulation of air and to hasten drying. If blocks are laid into a structure before their core has dried, when the final shrinkage does take place, it makes itself evident in spaces opening up between blocks and in a slight vertical settling of the walls. Though this is not too serious in a kiln where the blocks are laid up with a thin fireclay/sand mortar, in the walls of a permanent structure late shrinkage can break the bond between block and mortar and weaken the building.

The kiln I am going to describe was initiated by a group of students and was designed with their very specific ideals in mind. Number one student, "I want it to be a good size for a potter starting out on his own." Number two student, "The cost of materials can't be too high." Number three, "I'd like to be able to fire it for free."

The answer to what is a good-size kiln came slowly from a discussion of what a potter plans to fire in his kiln, how many people would be working to fill it, how frequently it would be fired, and could this kiln produce enough ware to return a livable income. The students compromised on a plan which also took into consideration the second point—the cost of bricks to build the structure and the cost of shelves to fill it.

A theoretical kiln emerged on paper. It was to have an interior of 36 cubic feet to be filled by two part-time potters, or one full-time, producing a mixture of handbuilt and thrown ware. Firing would be scheduled twice a month—frequently enough to get out quick orders and test results, but not so often that the process would monopolize studio time needed to produce the next kilnload. Hopefully the returns would pay the bills.

To keep initial expenses down, earthen blocks were to be used on the outside layer and hard firebricks, instead of soft bricks or ceramic fiber, on the interior. Since "free" fuels were postulated, any future saving from more effective insulation was a moot question. The fuels chosen were wood and drainoil. The former dictated a specific firebox design with grates and ashpit. The design of the oil burner (modified pipe) would allow flexibility so if circumstances changed, diesel or propane could be easily substituted.

Were the kiln to be fired regularly with commercial fuels, I would have recommended building it larger. A 100-cubic-foot kiln will burn only one-third more diesel than a 25-cubic-foot one, while firing four times as many pots. Almost without exception, a potter's second kiln is bigger than his first one.

The students added two last-minute preconditions: the kiln should fire to cone 10 and be able to be fired as a salt kiln. The reason for the first was the simplicity of glaze composition, particularly in the context of using local, natural materials. And remember, once it is firmly established the cone 10 habit is as hard to break as bisquing.

The desire for a salt kiln was rooted in students thinking, "In my own studio I probably can't afford the luxury of a self-destructive kiln. Let's do it now with school equipment!" That reasoning was clear and straightforward.

To accommodate the rigors of high temperature and sodium attack, we ordered new 2600° F. (1430° C.) firebricks. Once in place these were painted with a thick wash of alumina and kaolin, 1:1. Then the kiln was fired twice to cone 10, without salt, in order to "seal" the brick surface. For convenience and quicker salt vaporization, two ports were designed to fit into the wall, high above the firebox.

The students had decided a loading area of about a cubic yard would be a realistic starting point for their career. To establish the further proportions and details before starting construction, kiln building maxims were culled from literature in the field, folklore, superstition, and my experience. As it should be, the teacher was their last resort. Sister Magdalen

Mary once wrote, "The need is not how-to-do-it schools, but how-to-get-along-without-school schools."[16]

Their final list of principles sounded rigid, but in application maxims were bent or broken as the kiln went up:

(1) *Plan the kiln so that it can be constructed using only standard-size full and half-bricks.* Cutting odd shapes wastes time and bricks. In practice: purchased American size, straight firebricks—9 x 4½ x 2½ inches. Cut in half—4½ x 4½ x 2½ inches. All width and depth dimensions were divisible by 4½.

(2) *The interior volume should approximate a cube.* This shape is the most practical to heat evenly. In practice: 36 inches deep by 40½ inches wide by 52 inches high, including the rise of the arch. The eccentric height deviation was to accommodate tall pieces, and caused the top of the kiln to fire cooler than the bottom. This was corrected in the second firing by adding a three-brick-high (13½ inches) bag-wall on the edge of the grate.

(3) *Multiples of standard-sized kiln shelves should fit in the loading area, i.e.,* plan the kiln to fit shelves and not vice versa. In practice: the 27 x 36-inch loading platform held four 12 x 18-inch shelves per level.

(4) *The area of the grate should be one-third that of the loading area.* In practice: grate measured 9 x 36 inches—324 square inches; loading platform 27 x 36 inches—972 square inches.

(5) *The area of the base of the chimney should equal that of the grate.* In practice: grate 9 x 36 inches—324 square inches; stack 18 x 18 inches—324 square inches. This was not really important in a forced-air kiln. Similarly the height of the stack was not critical and stopped just above head level. Its function was simply to evacuate fumes, not create a draft.

(6) *The sum of the area of the flue openings should equal that of the burner ports.* What goes in, must come out. In practice: flues totaled 9½ x 10 inches—95 square inches; burner ports totaled 8 x 10 inches—80 square inches. Further constriction of the exits was manipulated with the dampers.

87. A foundation of cement, sand, and gravel (1:2:3) was poured and allowed to cure. The pad (a), approximately 6 inches thick, gave a level surface to work on and insurance against uneven settling once the kiln was built. Firebricks weigh between 7.6 and 8.4 pounds apiece. Six thousand pounds of these, plus the earthen blocks at 17 pounds each, placed a total of over 7.5 tons on the concrete slab. The floor/wall plan (b) was laid out and squared up.

In the tub (c) a dipping mortar was mixed for use as a leveling medium when the wall bricks were laid. One part fireclay was blended dry with one part sand, then enough water was added so that the soupy mixture would just barely float a brick. Such inert mortar is cheaper than the commercial, heat-setting varieties and is appreciated later when you decide to build a larger kiln and wish to separate and salvage the old kiln bricks.

88. As the firebrick walls rose, the earth blocks followed a few courses behind. One of the opposing dampers is visible (a). Firebricks line the openings at the door (b) and the fireboxes (c) and (d). This layer protected the blocks from flame impinging on them and possibly melting their surface. The ashpit (e) was not lined, because any heat escaping at that level would be considerably below melting temperature.

89. The subfloor (a) was two firebricks thick for insulation and to avoid damaging the concrete slab. A solid brick platform (b) three bricks higher served as the base of the loading area. This platform was constructed solid, rather than hollow, and slotted because the kiln was to be fired as a salt kiln. We did not want to allow the corrosive vapors to undermine it. Four-and-a-half-inch channels (c) bordering three sides allowed for flame circulation.

As mentioned earlier, the bag-wall (d) was later raised five bricks higher, *e.g.*, 12½ inches. Openings 4½ inches wide were left clear at both ends of this wall.

Soap bricks, 9 x 2¼ x 2½ inches, functioned as a grate (e). The fluxing action of wood ash, drainoil contaminants, and salt necessitated chipping and replacing individual bars from time to time.

90. Level walls were given closer attention as they neared the height where the arch form would rest. Two salting ports (a) and (b) were built in high enough for convenience when feeding them and low enough for eye safety when the hot salt spits and pops.

91. A plywood arch form (a), covered with ⅛-inch masonite, was nailed together and put in place where it was supported by the back wall and the corners of the front wall. Wedges cut from ¼-inch lath were placed under each of the four corners.

After the principles were translated into dimensions, we figured a rough estimate of how many firebricks would be needed. Bricklayers calculate that one square foot of wall or floor requires the following number of bricks:

a wall 4½ inches thick takes 6.4 bricks
a wall 9 inches thick takes 12.8 bricks

The 750 ordered for this kiln provided us with a generous surplus for shelf supports, bag-wall adjustments, etc. By not building the traditional nine-inch wall, the cost of another 650 to 700 was saved. Substituted in place of these firebricks were 550 earthen blocks made by the students. The larger measurements of the block (11½ x 5½ x 4 inches) explain the smaller total.

92. After the firebricks were laid on the form, angle irons (a) were placed on the four corners of the kiln, channel irons (b) in back of the arch, and this frame was tightened. The wedges were knocked loose. The form slid out, permitting completion of the front and back walls. Finally, the second course, the earthen blocks, were laid on the arch.

93. A seasoned, wood/drainoil kiln firing. The front burner port and ashpit openings were plugged and bricked up (a) after the wood fire heated the firebox to red heat. The oil storage tank was adjacent to the rear of this kiln so the drip burner was inserted in the rear port. The rear ashpit was blocked to keep excess air from cooling the firebox.

94. Close-up of clay in the ground. (*Ron Moroni*)

STALKING WILD MATERIALS

Finding Clay

Digging clay, grinding local rock for glazes, and gathering fuel are tasks as intrinsic to the early history of pottery as single-firing, and today about as common in practice. Ancient kiln sites are always unearthed in locations that were near either a plentiful source of fuel, a forest or a coal bed, or on top of a large deposit of clay. If resources ran low, and the demand for ware was still high, the potter left his kiln where it was and went out searching for materials. Evidence is inconclusive but probably most of the transported supplies were bartered for or purchased.

There are court records in England that tell other stories of our enterprising predecessors who shopped at night. In 1448, Staffordshire potters Richard and William Adams were fined for digging clay from the middle of the road between Sneyd and Burslem. A hundred years later a group of British potters were hauled into court and punished for digging holes in the Latton town common and not filling them back up. Staffordshire passed a law in 1604 threatening potters with a 6s.8d. fine if they were caught digging holes under city walls and not filling them in "well and sufficiently."

We happen to live in an era when the average student of ceramics learns first that clay comes moist in a plastic bag, prepaid. A 100-pound sack of feldspar can be purchased for less than the price of two six-packs of beer. Potters get arrested, but for victimless crimes unrelated to

95. Road cut, Nevada State Highway 11. (*Valerie Parks*)

our profession. Potters' studios are everywhere in times when clay and glaze materials can be casually ordered and then transported and delivered thousands of miles from the source. The costs are not great either. If figured per pot, they seldom total more than two percent of a fair retail price.

"So why go to the trouble of digging clay?"

I do for the same reasons you might plant a vegetable garden or go stream fishing. When I started, I told myself how much money I was going to save; in the end I told others how much I had gained in intangibles. I spoke at length of the value accrued in personal growth —returning to basics, understanding folk pottery, relating more closely with the environment, reacting against ceramic supply supermarkets, getting exercise, loving adventures. These are not the justifications of a pragmatist: in the twentieth century, romantics dig clay.

Since the beginning I have never been disappointed in the search. I look upon the enterprise as a healthy, spiritual quest rather than a trip to the thrift shop. The many hours spent shoveling clay into burlap sacks, dragging them to the pickup truck, slaking down and working up the clay are research for my mind and body. I do not always dig my own clay, but on summer mornings when I do, I always enjoy the act.

Finding the raw material is not hard, as it is estimated that at least 80 percent of the earth's crust is clay. When I am out driving, I check the scars where a road cuts through the side of a hill (Fig. 95), and the settlings in adjacent drainage ditches; walking the river fishing, I sample the eroded banks for outcroppings that feel like clay.

A sure way to discover clay in a new area is to ask a small kid in the neighborhood. If clay is around, he has had his hands in it. John Lawrence and Ann Verdcourt wrote in *Ceramic Review* of their emigration from Great

Britain to New Zealand and the search for clay there: "It was a schoolboy of eleven years old who eventually found us the position of what proved to be one of the best and biggest deposits of first-class stoneware clay in the North Island."[17]

My experience on arriving in Tuscarora closely paralleled theirs. Though at the time my guide was full-grown, she had played out her childhood in the gullies and on the tailing piles surrounding the town. She led me to the foundations of an old placer mill that sat in the center of what proved to be one of the best and biggest deposits of red earthenware clay in Elko County.

In searching for clay, a knowledge of earth sciences would seem to be a prerequisite. As it turns out, field geologists come in a distant second behind children. My personal experience has been that scientists are friendly enough, and want to help, but the problem develops that they see clay in the mind rather than the hand.

On two occasions geologists made the overture of coming to my aid by offering to run free analyses of some local clays, a red and a white earthenware. Samples were first subjected to electrodiffraction and these results came out:

	Red	White
kaolinite	60%–70%	10%–15%
illite	10%–20%	70%–80%
quartz	5%–10%	10%–15%
chlorite	5%–10%	—

The second test was qualitative, assessing the metallic content:

	Red	White
copper	.007	.009
silver	.081	—
zinc	.035	.016
cadmium	.004	—
lead	.032	.026
arsenic	.013	.002
antimony	.005	—
iron	2.900	4.500
cobalt	.004	—
nickel	.006	.008
rubidium	.010	.027
barium	.1700	.054
strontium	.014	.008
titanium	.240	.300
zirconium	.026	.029
manganese	.037	—
yttrium	.010	.009
columbium	—	.003
uranium	—	.005

96. Digging clay. (*Ron Moroni*)

97. Clay deposit. (*Ron Moroni*)

Years later the geologist who ran the second test confessed that had any of the percentages of the precious metals been high enough he would have felt obligated to his company to jump my claim.

The results of both of these tests, in their original form, are framed and hang on the wall in the studio. I point them out to visitors who ask, "What's in your clay? Anything special about it?"

Actually you can only assess the value of new clay on your own terms, potters' terms. If it is wet and sticky, and plastic enough to roll a coil or pinch out a crude pot, you tentatively label this clay. At least it is soil containing a relatively high percentage of clay. It could work. Where the ground is dry, look for an open area laced with a network of cracks, the evidence plastic clay leaves when it shrinks (Fig. 97).

Other preliminary considerations before taking samples back to the studio are: (1) Is the deposit contaminated with an excess of rocks or sand? If so, to free the clay, long hours of processing could be required. I would look for a cleaner deposit. (2) How large is the deposit? If the clay occurs only in a small pocket, your time will be wasted experimenting with it. (3) Who owns the land where you discovered the clay? Remember, potters can still get arrested for trespassing.

Only by firing clay samples can you learn the temperature range, degree of vitrification, color, and what unseen contamination may be present. The first test pot should be fired on a broken piece of kiln shelf, or nesting in another pot, just in case this test clay turns to glaze. Surface clays are often low-fire and predictably deform or melt above cone 1. If one does, put the sample aside for future testing as a slip glaze.

A clay test that comes out of a firing whole should be broken in half to check for vitrification. Note the degree of difficulty in breaking it. Put one of the rough edges against your tongue to get an idea of the porosity and a clue to whether or not you might wish to add a flux to tighten up the body. If need be, follow this with further test firing using five percent increments of flux (talc for low-fire clay and feldspar for high-fire).

In situ, clay may be seen that is green, blue, yellow, black, gray, or white, and yet all of them could fire to the same color. My white earthenware fired out medium brown. The colorant in unfired clay is mostly decomposed organic matter which smells bad when you work with the clay and subsequently burns out in the kiln. The prime determinate of fired color, nine times out of ten, is the amount of iron in a clay.

Serious problems arise when limestone or sulfur are in clay. The former reacts after firing in the same ugly manner as fragments of plaster of paris. If any particles (60-mesh or larger) are entrapped in the clay and the pot is later moistened, this triggers the process of hydration. Each particle of lime expands with a force greater than the strength of clay, thus pockmarking the surface of the pot. Even humid weather can provide enough moisture to set off the destruction. If this happens to your clay, the best resolution is to look for another source. For this reason, the Tuscarora white clay was abandoned.

Clay with sulfur is also best forgotten. Become suspicious of its presence in a new clay if your old reliable glazes fire dull, dry, wrinkled, pinholed, or blistered.

Wild clay frequently needs domestication, *e.g.*, what you find may not behave the way you want it to. Though there are clays that can be worked straight from the ground, they are rare. A clay body should be blended to suit your plans. I prefer more grog in handbuilding clay than in throwing clay; a smoother clay for plates than for planters; a stronger fabric in bowls than in mugs, etc. Therefore, in mixtures where I need more wet strength, or want texture, I add nonplastics such as grog, sand, and mica. To increase plasticity I add ball clay. The fired color can be lightened or darkened by varying the percentage of iron-bearing clay.

The technology employed in Tuscarora for processing local dry clay into a moist clay body strikes most visitors as being underdeveloped, but I am proud that it has evolved only to the highest level required for the job. The red earthenware is relatively clean, with a tolerable amount of sand, a few stray pebbles, and an assortment of innocuous twigs and roots. The steps to refine it are basic.

Clay is spread out to dry in the sun. Dry clay slakes down faster and results in fewer hard lumps. Later it is shoveled into buckets, half full of water, and left undisturbed for several hours. Bits of wood have the opportunity to float to the top, while rocks and pebbles sink.

The slurry is mixed by hand, lumps squeezed out, and the flotsam is scummed from the surface. At this time any additives, such as ball clay, are mixed in.

98. Unglazed raku bottle, by Jeff Schlanger, made from local white earthenware. Height 17 inches (43.2 cm.). Note limestone pop-outs. (*Valerie Parks*)

99. Laying slurry out to dry. (*Ron Moroni*)

The contents of the bucket (with the exception of the bottom inch) is scooped or ladled into drying troughs. These have been prepared by digging bowl-shaped depressions in the ground and lining them with cloth. Finally the slurry is smoothed and left to stiffen (Fig. 99).

When the clay reaches wedging consistency, it is worked into large balls and stored under plastic for at least two days. Seldom does the clay have more than two weeks to age before it is used up. Further aging would do much to improve the plasticity.

100. An arrangement for drying clay in a wet climate. The slurry is elevated on a screen covered with cloth and supported by bricks. An A-frame roof is covered with plastic. Studio of Peter Dick.

By coincidence these steps are close to those observed by Dr. Plot in his *Natural History of Staffordshire*, 1686: ". . . they prepare the clay by steeping it in water in a square pit, till it be of a due consistence; they then bring it to their beating board, where they beat it with a long spatula till it be well mixed; then being made into great squarish rolls, it is brought to the wageing board, where it is slit into thin flat pieces with a wire, and the least stones or gravel pikt out of it; this being done they wage it, i.e. knead or mould it like bread, and make it into round balls proportioned to their work, and then tis brought to the wheel, and formed as the workman sees good."

A concession to modernity was added to my

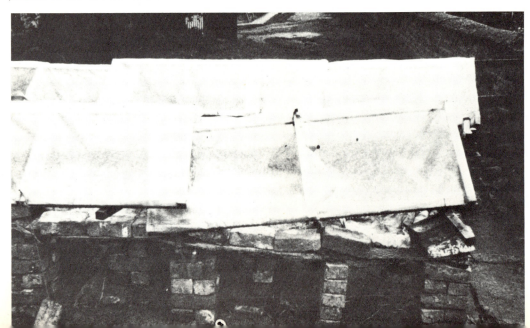

equipment after the summer of 1967 when Paul Soldner welded for me the prototype of a bicycle-powered barrel separator (Fig. 101). Now, if the need arises, I am able to further refine the local clay into a very smooth body. Basically the machine is a screen that rejects large particles and channels the fine on into the drying pit.

To use the separator it is necessary to mix dry clay into a thick slip rather than a slurry, then pour it into the trough located directly behind the bicycle seat. The rider pedals slowly along. Since the barrel-screen is slightly lower at the opposite end, all the lumps, pebbles, and sand (too large to leak through the 30-mesh screen) come bouncing out the opening. Smooth, clean slip drips in the collecting pan which empties into a drainpipe and flows to the drying pit (Fig. 102). Of course this slip takes considerably longer to dry than the slurry.

Finding Glaze Materials

In finding glaze materials adult knowledge is more helpful than childhood instincts or memories. Geologists, in their quest for gold and silver, are forever dropping off on my doorstep sample sacks of materials they have incidentally discovered and hope might be useful at

101. Soldner bicycle-powered separator: (a) trough; (b) barrel screen; (c) collecting pan; (d) drain pipe; (e) drying pit. (*Ron Moroni*)

102. Slip in the foreground, slurry in the background. (*Ron Moroni*)

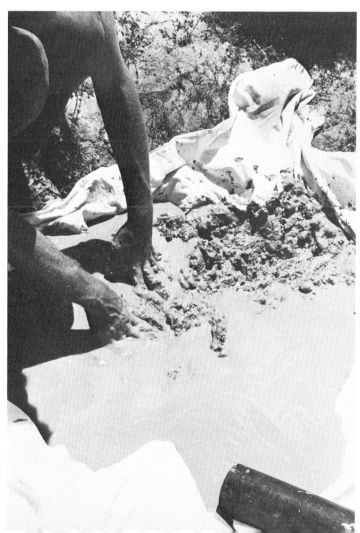

least to me: feldspar, volcanic ash, calcite, copper and iron ore, talc, and dolomite.

A reservoir of information is inside the Tuscarora Tavern. Almost any evening I can walk in and pull up a stool between an eighty-year-old prospector and some twenty-two-year-old geology graduate. The prospector knows every pile of rocks within a 20-mile radius of town, and loves to talk on and on about each. The geologist is eager to learn about the countryside and is proud of his ability to identify any samples I have collected. Such a consultation costs me one round of drinks.

The details from my environment do not have a wide applicability, but a methodology relying on curiosity and friendship works anywhere: (1) Write the chairman of the Geology Department at your state college or university. He or she may have a graduate student around who will label your mineral samples for no charge. From time to time show your gratitude with a gift of pottery. (2) Check out any businesses in your area that work with earth materials—granite and marble quarries, gravel pits, cement plants. All these have wastes that are worth testing and the owners are usually happy to have you haul some away. Fire these samples and then proceed to line blends and triaxials.

The artist Kurt Schwitters in the 1920s walked the streets of Berlin with his head down looking at the sidewalks for litter, the raw material of his collages. Today if I were a city potter, I would think about adapting his instincts to my ceramics. Could gutter sweepings from the south side of Lafayette Square make a glaze? How would that differ from what I could collect at Dupont Circle, or the east side of Wisconsin Avenue between M and N streets? Could I trade pots with a waiter in a Georgetown barbecue in return for a regular supply of hickory ash?

I might sweep out the brass filings from under the key duplicator in a hardware store for a source of copper; scrape iron rust from under the fender of a neighbor's car; take dangerous chances by melting lead plates from used car batteries to brew lead oxide (this unhealthy practice is recorded in France as late as World War II); and finally at the end of a day justify long walks down Rock Creek and up the bank of the Potomac River collecting samples.

My problem has never been finding materials as much as finding the means to reduce them from their natural state to powder. The cost of the right equipment is out of the reach of a studio potter. To grind a feldspathic rock requires a hammer mill or a jaw crusher to break it down from the size of a fist to that of a pea. Then a pulverizer or a ball mill to crush it the rest of the way to 200-mesh. Unless you have use of such machinery it is wise to narrow your search to soft ingredients that break up with just a mortar and pestle and a ball mill.

Some materials such as granite can be softened by calcining, *i.e.*, firing the rocks to red heat in a kiln. On cooling, the samples are so friable that they can be crumbled by hand and then easily ball-milled to a powder. In stream beds nature exhibits the same grinding action of a ball mill. The silt and sand in the bottom of pools, or tucked back in an eddy, can be included in a glaze with no process more complex than sifting through a fine screen.

Some Simple Glazes

Through experiments I have been led to a number of simple, yet reliable glazes. The following I mix by volume, in large batches, and use regularly:

Mud Puddle
cone 10 reduction
the chips that curl up after the rain
    evaporates   10 parts
dolomite   1 part
    Apply to dry clay. Lustrous brown.

Half-and-Half
cone 10 reduction
ball-milled sand   1 part
sifted sagebrush ash, 80-mesh   1 part
    Apply to dry clay. Tenmoku.

103. Dried mud.

Cement
cone 8–10 reduction

ball-milled Portland cement (Either that which has been washed out of a cement truck, and dried on the ground, or fresh from a sack, mixed with water, frozen, and thawed. Neither of these will later turn to concrete in the glaze bucket.)	1 part
low-fire plastic clay	2 parts
sifted softwood ash, 80-mesh	1 part

Apply to dry clay. Snakeskin texture. The iron content of the low-fire clay sets the color of the glaze from yellow-green to brown.

Two Gerstley to One Anything
cone 06–04 raku or oxidation

Gerstley borate (colemanite)	2 parts
"anything" (feldspar—clear crackle; ash—pale green; copper ore—bright green or bright red; etc.)	1 part

Apply to dry clay.

I do not kid myself about wild materials someday supplanting the necessity for ordering supplies. They could, though I resist having my options narrowed. My local ingredients are richer in impurities, and I often think the glazes come out lovelier; but the issue is debatable. The value of the search is pleasure, and the value from using what I discover is that of defining the personality of my work more specifically.

I gradually developed a respect for the details of my environment as I came to understand them. An awareness of where you are gives valuable clues to who you are and urges you on to solve greater mysteries.

For a long time I have been fascinated by compression—shortcuts, shorthand, secret codes, poems, metamorphic rocks, and thrown pottery. I recommend techniques—glazing with local materials, erecting dirt kilns, firing with discarded oil and applying glaze to raw clay—because they are related means of investing an object with energies.

In how you treat that piece of clay lies your only clear and obvious artifact.

NOTES

Chapter 1.

1. Hsiang Ju Lin and Tsuifeng Lin, *Chinese Gastronomy* (New York: Pyramid, 1972), p. 173.

Chapter 2.

2. R. L. Hobson, *Chinese Pottery and Porcelain* (New York: Dover, 1976), p. 92.
3. Alan Caiger-Smith, *Tin-Glaze Pottery* (London: Faber & Faber, 1973; and Atlantic Highlands, N.J.: Humanities Press, 1973), p. 204.
4. Harry Davis, "An Historical Review of Art, Commerce and Craftsmanship," *Studio Potter*, Vol. 6, No. 1, p. 8.
5. Michael Cardew, *Pioneer Pottery* (London: Longmans, Green, 1969; and New York: St. Martin's, 1969), p. 130.

Chapter 3.

6. Aurèle La Rocque, trans., *The Admirable Discourses of Bernard Palissy*, 1580 (Urbana: University of Illinois, 1957).

Chapter 4.

7. Sōetsu Yanagi, *The Unknown Craftsman* (Tokyo: Kodansha International, 1973), pp. 120-121.

Chapter 5.

8. From an American Gas Association article, "Energy Utilization Efficiency of Major Home Appliances" (October 1973).
9. From Charles Hendricks and Don Pilcher, in "The Pollution Aspects of Salt Glaze Firing," *Salt Glaze Ceramics* (New York: American Crafts Council, 1972), p. 24.
10. *Road and Track* (April 1976), editorial.
11. From R. A. Fromme, "Letters," *Studio Potter*, Vol. 5, No. 2, p. 90.
12. From Dennis Parks, "Reply to R. A. Fromme's Letter," *Studio Potter*, Vol. 5, No. 2, p. 90.
13. From Dale White Toyota Garage, Elko, Nevada. Tested by Roland Di Sanza, Kennecott Copper Corporation, Ely, Nevada. (December 21, 1976.)
14. From west of the Navaho Mine, Tuscarora, Nevada. Tested by Spectrographic Analytical Laboratory, Denver, Colorado. (August 22, 1969.)
15. Converted from analysis in Roger J. Williams, *Nutrition Against Disease* (New York: Pitman, 1971), p. 305.

Chapter 6.

16. Sister Mary Magdalen, "Art Education and the Order of Things," *Education*, Vol. 77, No. 3 (November 1956), p. 5.
17. John Lawrence and Ann Verdcourt, "A Pottery in New Zealand," *Ceramic Review*, No. 52 (July-August 1978), p. 6.

BIBLIOGRAPHY

BOOKS

Burkhardt, Charles H. *Domestic and Commercial Oil Burners.* New York: McGraw-Hill, 1969.

Caiger-Smith, Alan. *Tin-Glaze Pottery.* London: Faber & Faber, 1973; and Atlantic Highlands, N.J.: Humanities Press, 1973.

Cardew, Michael. *Pioneer Pottery.* London: Longmans, Green, 1969; and New York: St. Martin's, 1969.

Cary, Joyce. *The Horse's Mouth.* London: Penguin, 1948; and New York: Harper & Row, 1965.

Cooper, Emmanuel. *A History of Pottery.* London: Longman's, Green, 1972; and New York: St. Martin's, 1973.

Cooper, Ronald G. *English Slipware Dishes 1650–1850.* London: Alex Tiranti, 1968.

Evison, Vera I., Hodges, H., and Hurst, J. G., eds. *Medieval Pottery from Excavations.* London: John Baker, 1974; and New York: St. Martin's, 1975.

Field, Edwin M. *Oil Burners.* Indianapolis: Audel, 1973.

Hamer, Frank. *The Potter's Dictionary of Materials and Techniques.* New York: Watson-Guptill, 1975.

Hobson, R. L. *Chinese Pottery and Porcelain.* New York: Dover, 1976.

La Rocque, Aurèle, trans. *The Admirable Discourses of Bernard Palissy,* 1580. Urbana: University of Illinois, 1957.

Lawrence, W. G. *Ceramic Science for the Potter.* Philadelphia: Chilton, 1972.

Leach, Bernard. *A Potter's Book.* Hollywood-by-the-Sea, Fla.: Transatlantic Arts, Inc., 1965.

Lewenstein, Eileen, and Cooper, Emmanuel, eds. *The Revised and Enlarged Ceramic Review Book of Glaze Recipes.* London: Ceramic Review, 1978.

Lin, Hsiang Ju, and Lin, Tsuifeng. *Chinese Gastronomy.* New York: Pyramid, 1972.

Medley, Margaret. *The Chinese Potter.* New York: Scribners, 1976.

Nelson, Glenn C. *Ceramics: A Potter's Handbook.* New York: Holt, Rinehart and Winston, 1971.

Olsen, Frederick L. *The Kiln Book.* Bassett, Calif.: Keramos Books, 1973.

Parmelee, Cullen W. *Ceramic Glazes.* Boston: Cahners, 1973.

Plot, Dr. *Natural History of Staffordshire,* 1686. As quoted in *Tin-Glaze Pottery* (see Caiger-Smith).

Rhodes, Daniel. *Kilns: Design, Construction and Operation.* Philadelphia: Chilton, 1968.

Troy, Jack. *Salt-Glazed Ceramics.* New York: Watson-Guptill, 1977.

Yanagi, Sōetsu. *The Unknown Craftsman.* Tokyo: Kodansha International, 1973.

ARTICLES AND PAMPHLETS

Adobe Construction Methods. Davis, Calif.: University of California College of Agriculture, 1964.

Building with Adobe and Stabilized-Earth Blocks. Washington, D.C.: Department of Agriculture, 1965.

"Ceramactivities: Terra Sigillata." *Ceramics Monthly* (January 1978).

Cowan, Roy. "Oil-Fired Kilns." *Pottery Quarterly,* Vol. 10, No. 38.

———. "Oil-Fired Kilns 2." *Pottery Quarterly,* Vol. 10, No. 39.

Curtis, Suzi. "Raw Glazed Reduced Stoneware." *Pottery Quarterly,* Vol. 11, No. 43.

Davis, Harry. "An Historical Review of Art, Commerce and Craftsmanship." *Studio Potter,* Vol. 6, No. 1.

Dick, Peter. "A Woodfired Kiln at Coxwold Pottery." *Ceramic Review,* No. 47 (September–October 1977).

Earth for Homes. Washington, D.C.: Department of Housing and Urban Affairs, 1955.

Hendricks, Charles, and Pilcher, Don. "The Pollution Aspects of Salt Glaze Firing." *Salt Glaze Ceramics.* New York: American Crafts Council, 1972.

Hopper, Robin. "Glazes—Try It and See." *Ceramic Review,* No. 37 (January–February 1976).

Hyman, Sylvia. "Beads from Raku-Fired Egyptian Paste." *Ceramics Monthly* (April 1974).

Ihrman, Phyllis. "Single-Fire Glazes, Part I." *Ceramics Monthly* (October 1976).

———. "Single-Fire Glazes, Part II." *Ceramics Monthly* (November 1976).

Irving, Tam. "On Using Naturally Occurring Materials in Glazes." *Studio Potter*, Vol. 4, No. 1.

Kiefer, Charles, and Allibert, A. "Pharaonic Blue Ceramics." *Archaeology* (April 1971).

Lawrence, John, and Verdcourt, Ann. "A Pottery in New Zealand." *Ceramic Review*, No. 52 (July-August 1978).

"Letters." *Studio Potter*, Vol. 5, No. 2.

Magdalen Mary, Sister. "Art Education and the Order of Things." *Education*, Vol. 77, No. 3 (November 1956).

Noble, Joseph Veach. "The Technique of Egyptian Faience." *American Journal of Archaeology* (October 1969).

Parks, Dennis. "Dust Glazing." *Ceramics Monthly* (October 1977).

———. "Fired Free." *Studio Potter*, Vol. 5, No. 1.

———. "One-Fire Glazing." *Studio Potter*, Vol. 3, No. 1.

———. "Report from China." *Ceramics Monthly* (June 1978).

———. "Single Fire Glazing." *Ceramic Review*, No. 46 (July-August 1977).

———. "Single Glaze Firing." *New Zealand Potter*, Vol. 19, No. 1 (Autumn 1977).

———. "Tales of Woe." *Studio Potter*, Vol. 7, No. 1.

———. "Tuscarora." *The Goodfellow Review of Crafts*, Vol. 6, No. 2 (April-May 1978).

Soldner, Paul. "Workshop with Paul Soldner: Firing with Oil." *Craft Horizons*, Vol. 28, No. 1 (January-February 1968).

Stannard, Ann. "Drip Feed Oil/Water Burner." *Studio Potter*, Vol. 3, No. 1.

SOURCES OF HARD-TO-FIND EQUIPMENT

The Cinva-Ram Block Press
Write: c/o Bellows-Valvair
200 West Exchange St.
Akron, Ohio 44309

The Kutrieb Waste Oil Room Heater
Write: c/o Lenan Enterprises Inc.
P.O. Box 94
Milton, Wis. 53563

INDEX

Italicized page numbers indicate the location of photos and line-art illustrations.

Adams, Richard and William, 95
Alexander, William, *terra sigillata* recipes, 55-56
Allen, Jim, 19
   glaze recipes, 45
alumina, 13, 14, 15, 27, 37, 49, 50, 90
ash, *see* glazes, ash

ball clay, 15, 16, 17, 27, 28, 29, 33, 49, 99
barium, 15, 16
Bean, Bennett, 24
   low-fire plate, *25*
bentonite, 17, 29, 33, 34
binders, 21, 26, 28, 29
bisque
   history of firing, 10-14
   raw glaze vs. bisque, 17-18
Booth, Enoch, 11
borax, 14, 51
boron, 15
Boyden, Frank, carp vase, *29*
Braverman, Max, 34
burners, oil, *see* oil burners

Caiger-Smith, Alan, quoted, 11
calcium, 15
Capes, Rosemary, glaze recipes, 46
carbon, 28, 56-57, 79
Cardew, Michael, 13
   quoted, 17
Chinese pottery, 10, 11, 12, 13, *24*, 36-37, *37, 56*
Cinva-Ram Block Press, *83, 84-94, 86, 87, 88, 89,* 108
clay
   body relationship to glaze, 17-18, 27, 28-33
   native (local), 16, 34, 95-101, *95, 97, 98*; native, analysis, 63, 97; native, processing, 99-101, *100, 101*; native, testing, 98-99
   pH, 27-28
   problems, 27-28, 38, 99
   salt bodies, 47-49
   self-glazing, 53-56
Clorox, 21
cobalt, 16, 49

Cohen, Burt, 78
colemanite, 14, 16
copper, 16, 52, 102
Cornell, David, 27
   diagram, 10
   glaze recipes, 43-44
   stoneware plate, *31*
crankcase oil, *see* drainoil
Craven, J. D., salt-glazed stoneware churn, *52*
Creitz, Bill, 33
Curtis, Suzi, 34
   glaze recipes, 39, 40-41

Davies, John, glaze recipe, 41
Davis, Harry, quoted, 13
decoration, 13, 52, 53
   sgraffito, 36-37, *37*
   slip, 49-50
   terra nigra, 56-57, *56*
De Kooning, Willem, quoted, 66
dextrine, 21, 24, 26
Dick, Peter, 33, 35, 71, 100
   bowls, *33*
diesel, 52, 58-81, *77,* 90
   Btu, 60
   see also oil *and* oil burners
dirt
   in glaze, 25, 34
   use of, in kiln building, 82-94
Dodd, Mike, glaze recipe, 42
dolomite, 15, 16, 33
drainoil, *7,* 52, 58-81, *59, 76, 77,* 90
   aesthetics, 65-66
   analysis, 63
   Btu, 60
   economy, 60
   source, 6, 8
   system, 74-76, *75*
draw rings, 51
Dwight, John, "Lydia Dwight," *48*

Egyptian paste, 13, 14, 53-55, *53*
   recipes, 54-55
Elliott, Fred, 6-7, 58

Evans, Tony, 17-18
  glaze recipe, 39

Felberbaum, Alicia, Egyptian paste recipe, 54
feldspar, 13, 14, 15, 16, 17, 33, 49, 99
firebox, *see* kilns, firebox
firebricks, *see* kilns, firebricks
flint, 15, 16
flux, 13, 14, 15, 16, 28, 47, 49, 54, 98-99
Foster, John A., 32
  glaze recipes, 42
Frewin, Alan, glaze recipe, 39-40
frits, 16
fuel
  electricity, 58, 61, 63, 65
  gas, 52, 58-60, 61, 63, 64, 69-70, 71-72, 74, 79, 90
  kerosene, 59
  stove oil, 59
  wood, 52, 58, 59-60, 63, 65, 71, 72, 74, 79, 90
  see also diesel, drainoil, *and* oil

galena, 13, 25, *25*
Gardiner, Ray, glaze recipes, 40-41
glazes
  application, dry, 8, 17, 18, 19-32, 37, 38-39; application, leather-hard, 17, 18, 27, 29, 32-37, 38-39; application, wet, 18, 29, 32-37, 38-39
  ash, 13, 14, 16, 24, 25, *26*, 34, 41-42, 43
  composition, 8, 14-17
  definition, 13-14
  flaws, blistering, dunting, lifting, pinholing, shivering, 29; flaws, crawling, 11, 17, 21, 29, 34; flaws, flaking, 21, 28-29, 34; flaws, scuffing, 21
  formulae, Unity (Seger, Molecular or Empirical), 14, 15
  formulation, 14-17, 33-34, 42, 49
  history, 10-14
  lead, 13, 14, 25
  mixing, 20-21
  native materials, 101-4, *103*
  prepared, 14, 17, 25
  raw vs. bisque, 17
  reasons for, 12-13
  recipes, 16-17, 34, 38-46, 102, 104
  relationship to clay body, 17-18, 27, 28-33
  salt, 8-9, 13, 14, 47-53, 66; salt, English, 8; salt, German, 8, 13, 14, 49
  testing, 16, 17, 49 (*and see also* line blends *and* triaxials)
  tin, 10, 11, *11*
Green, John, glaze recipe, 40
grog, 27, 54, 99

Hendry, Ken, self-glazing clay recipes, 54-55
Hill, Steven, stoneware covered jar, *31*

Hobson, R. L., quoted, 10, 11
Holaday, Inez, burner, 71-72, 79
Holden, Andrew, 18
  glaze recipes, 43
Hopper, Robin, 16
Hsiang Ju Lin, quoted, 6
Hyman, Sylvia, Egyptian paste recipe, 54

Ihrman, Phyllis, 32, 34
  glaze recipes, 42, 45
  porcelain bottle with crystalline glaze, *32*
iron, 16, 28, 47, 51, 99, 102

Johnstone, Sandra, 18
  glaze recipes, 45
  loaded salt-glaze kiln, *51*
Judson, Carl, 33

kaolin, 15, 16, 17, 27, 28, 29, 33, 49, 50, 90
kaolin fibers, 82
Kilborn, Steve and Ann, glaze recipe, 40
kilns
  bagwalls, 78, 79, 91, *92*, 94
  building, 50, 71, 82-94, *83, 84, 91-94*; building, principles, 91, 94; building, use of earthen blocks, 82-94 (*and see also* Cinva-Ram Block Press)
  designs, 8, 77-79, 90-94; designs, cross draft, 66-67, 72, 78; designs, down-draft, 78, 79; designs, up-draft, 72, 77, 78, 79
  firebox, 59, 60, 65, 68, 69, 71, 72, 73, 76, 77, 78, 79, 90, *92*, 94
  firebricks, 47, 50-51, 78, 79, 82, 84, 90, 91, 94
  firing schedule, 37-38, 79-81
  loading, 37, 50-51
  natural draft, 72-73
  oil-fired, *65, 71, 75*, 77-79, *77, 78, 80*, 82-94, *94*
  safety, 63-65
  salt, 9, 47, 50-53; salt, building, 90-94; salt, firing, 51-53
  wash, 50, 90
Kutrieb Waste Oil Room Heater, 76, 108

Lawrence, John, and Ann Verdcourt, 96-97
  quoted, 97
Leach, Bernard, 13
lead, 13, 14, 15, 25, 63, 102
limestone, 17, 99
line blends, 15, 102
lithium, 16
Lord, Andrew, "Round Black Set," *35*
Lykins, Jere
  floor plan of 60-cubic-foot kiln, *77*
  glaze recipes, 40, 46
  salt-glazed stoneware cup and saucer, *50*
  sixty-cubic-foot kiln, *65*

110

Mackey, Richard, glaze recipes, 40, 41
Maddox, Lynn
   glaze recipes, 40
   salt-glazed stoneware covered jar, *48*
magnesium, 15, 16
magnesium carbonate, 49
materials, native, 95-104
McMichael, Laurie and Anne, glaze recipe, 42-43
mica, 27, 48, 99

oil, 58-81
   Btu, 59, 60, 79
   characteristics, 58-60
   converting to, 66, 77-78
   ecology, 61-63
   flash point, 59-60, 69, 76
   problems, 60-65, 67; problems, clinkers, 65, 77, 79
   safety, 63-65
   viscosity, 59, 69, 76
   water, effect, 76-77
oil burners, 58-59, 66-81
   commercial, 78
   drip-feed pipe, 67-69, *68*, 73
   Holaday, 71-72, *72*, 79
   low-pressure orifice, 73-74, *74*; Denver, 73, *73*; New Soldner, 73, 74, *74*; New Zealand, 73, 74
   modified pipe, 58, *64*, 69, *69*, *75*, 79, 90
   propane/oil combination, 69-70, *70*
   stepladder or louvre, 72-73, *73*
   valves, heat sensitive, 64, 65
   weed, 66-67, *67*
   wood/oil combination, 71, *71*
once-firing, *see* single-firing
opacifiers, 16
opax, 16
oxides, 16, 22, 29, 47, 49

Palissy, Bernard, quoted, 38
Parmelee, Cullen W., 55
pit fire, 56-57
Pleydell-Bouverie, Katharine, glaze recipe, 41
Plot, Dr., quoted, 100
Portland cement
   in earthen blocks, 85, 86, 89-90
   in glaze, 25, 104
potassium, 16
Pousony, Valley, 12

quartz, 15

raku, *6*, 56-57, 66-67, *80*, *99*
Russum, Olin, 24

saggars, 12, 56, 57
salt-clay bodies, *see* clay, salt bodies

salt glaze, *see* glazes, salt
salt kiln, *see* kilns, salt
sand, 13, 15, 27, 48, 99
Seger, Hermann A., 14
sgraffito, decoration, 36-37, *37*
Shep, Larry, 36
   five-gallon planters, *36*
   glaze recipe, 46
silica, 13, 14, 15, 16, 17, 47, 49, 54
single-firing, 8, 17-18, 37-38, 58
   history, 10-14
   problems, 27
   schedule, 79-81
   variations, 47-57
Sister Mary Magdalen, quoted, 90-91
Skolnick-Simonson, Marcia and Don, glaze recipe, 46
slips, 22, 25, 26, 29, 36-37, 39, 40, 41, 42, 47, 55
   decoration, 49-50
   porcelain, 49
   terra sigillata, 55-56
soda, *see* sodium
soda ash, 27, 52
sodium, 13, 14, 16, 47, 49, 51, 52, 54, 90
   soda and sal soda, 52
Schlanger, Jeff, raku bottle, *99*
Sohngen, Peter, 19
   glaze recipes, 44-45
   stoneware plate, *19*
Soldate, Joe, 21
Soldner, Paul, 19
   barrel separator, 100-101, *101*
   burners, 67-68, 73-74, *74*
   glaze recipes, 39
Staffordshire, 100
   bisquing brought to, 11
   potters, 95
   tortoiseshell ware of Whieldon type, 10
stannous chloride, 52-53
sulfur, 99
sump oil, *see* drainoil
superpax, 16

talc, 99
teacher, role of, 6-7, 90-91
terra nigra, 56-57, *56*
terra sigillata, 55-56, *55*, *56*
Toft, Thomas, Lion Rampant dish, *14*
triaxials, 15-16, 102
Tuscarora, Nevada, 2, 3, 4, 9, 25, 56, 60, 86, 97, 99
Tuscarora Pottery School, 4-6, *38*, 75, 80

Valley, Andrée
   glaze recipes, 40, 41-42, 43
   "Kimberlite Pipe," *49*

Verdcourt, Ann, and John Lawrence, 96–97
   quoted, 97
Voulkos, Peter, 14–15

waste oil, *see* drainoil
wax resist, *23*, *37*
whiting, 16, 33, 49
Williams, Hank, song quoted, 3
Woodman, Betty
   glaze recipe, 39
   Italian earthenware vase, *30*
   "Raw-glazed ware waiting to go in kiln," *20*
   terra sigillata basket, *55*

Yanagi, Sōetsu, quoted, 57

zinc, 16, 33, 49
zircopax, 16

YOUR OWN GLAZE RECIPES

YOUR OWN GLAZE RECIPES

YOUR OWN GLAZE RECIPES

YOUR OWN GLAZE RECIPES

YOUR OWN GLAZE RECIPES

YOUR OWN GLAZE RECIPES